LVE
—— FOR A ——
LIFETIME

L♡VE

—— FOR A ——

LIFETIME

Daily Wisdom and Wit for a
Long and Happy Marriage

Mary Hance

TURNER
PUBLISHING COMPANY

Turner Publishing Company
4507 Charlotte Avenue, Suite 100
Nashville, TN 37209
Phone: (615)255-2665   Fax: (615)255-5081

Love for a Lifetime: Daily Wisdom and Wit for a Long and Happy Marriage

www.turnerpublishing.com

Cover design by Mike Penticost

Library of Congress Cataloging-in-Publication Data

Hance, Mary, 1953-
Love for a lifetime : daily wisdom and wit for a long and happy marriage / Mary
Morton Hance.
     p. cm.
ISBN 978-1-59652-805-5
1. Marriage--Miscellanea. 2. Man-woman relationships--Miscellanea. I. Title.
HQ734.H2597 2011
646.7'8--dc22

                              2010046715

Printed in the United States of America

11 12 13 14 15 16 17 18 — 0 9 8 7 6 5 4 3 2

To my husband, Bill
(yes, after twenty-nine years together he still makes me laugh
and feel good about life), and to our daughters, Elizabeth and
Anna, and their husbands, Chad and Santi, with the hope that
they will have long and truly happy and fulfilling marriages that
are supported by the boundless love, faith, patience, forgiveness,
and humor that are promoted in this book

Contents

Acknowledgments   *xi*

Introduction   *1*

The 365 Things   *3*

1. Advice from Friends   *3*
2. Advice from Readers   *8*
3. Celebrity Section   *129*
4. More Big-Name Advice   *135*
5. Married Fifty Years or More   *153*
6. Family Advice   *159*
7. Advice from Experts   *171*
8. Prayer for a Married Couple   *181*

Conclusion   *182*

Acknowledgments

Much of the material in this book first appeared in the Ms. Cheap column in the *Tennessean.* It is copyrighted by and used with the permission of the *Tennessean.*

A special thanks to my special friends Beth Stein, Beverly Keel, Jane Dubose, Mary Shelton, Barbara Sanders, Greer Broemel, and the Reverend Patricia Templeton, whose astute observations are incorporated into the first sixteen tips.

For the celebrity section, beginning at number 264, my good friend Beverly Keel married for the first time at age forty-one and was the celebrity columnist for the *Tennessean* at the time of her wedding. She and the *Tennessean* granted me permission to use the advice that some of Nashville's most famous names shared with her for her column on how to have a happy marriage.

Love suffers long and is kind;
love does not envy; love does not parade itself, is not puffed up;
does not behave rudely, does not seek its own, is not provoked,
thinks no evil; does not rejoice in iniquity, but rejoices in the truth;
bears all things, believes all things, hopes all things,
endures all things.

~1 Corinthians 13:4-7

Introduction

First of all, I must tell you that I am not any kind of marriage expert. Rather, I am an ordinary person juggling marriage, children, a few hobbies, and my work as a frugal consumer columnist for the *Tennessean* newspaper in Nashville. So you may wonder what on earth a cheapo columnist like me is doing writing about something as serious and complicated as marriage. Well, oddly enough, the idea for the book and much of the material actually did come out of my column.

It all started when our older daughter Elizabeth and her husband, Chad, were planning their wedding. As part of the pre-wedding hoopla, I asked some of my closest and oldest friends to share their best counsel for a happy marriage. I thought I would get the same old tried and true (albeit pretty mundane) stuff that you would expect at a bridal luncheon. But these friends bowled me over with their thoughtful and poignant pointers and observations.

I realized immediately that the things they said were valuable not just for people like our children who were embarking on the fresh adventure and challenge of marriage, but for all of us in various stages of our relationships. So, I solicited more advice from my newspaper readers and again was rewarded with so many insightful sharings that I wrote a column a year later, the same week of the wedding of our second daughter Anna to her husband, Santiago. I then widened the net and begged friends and relatives and fellow bloggers to contribute ideas. I read recommended books about marriage, I went online for ideas, and then I solicited suggestions and maxims from bona fide marriage and relationship counselors to round things out.

This book—this collection of advice for a long and happy marriage—is truly the result of wonderful sharing, reflecting, and collecting. For the most part, these 365 tips come from real people, just regular folks like you and me—some of whom have been married more than seventy years, and others who have been married only a few months. In addition, some of the thoughts come from people who have suffered through harrowing marriages and nasty divorces and have learned a few things along the way that they were willing to share. Some are really funny and some are really serious, but I think all of them are worth thinking about. The advice was limited to 365 bits of wisdom, to give you one thing, and in a few cases one short list of things, to think about every day in the calendar year.

I am deeply indebted to everyone who took the time to share ideas to make this book come to life. I loved hearing from so many of you who thanked me for inviting you to participate—saying it had been fun and uplifting for you and your spouse to talk and think about what has helped you to build and sustain your precious relationship. Some said they quizzed their "greatest generation" parents for sage advice and gained priceless insights from them.

And thank you all as readers. Of course, my highest hope is that you will come across a nugget or two—or maybe even more—of wisdom or practicality that will enhance and enrich your marriage. Please read and enjoy.

The 365 Things

Advice from Friends

As I said at the outset, the seeds for this book came from a group of my friends at a bridal luncheon, and I want to kick things off with their ideas for our little bride.

1

Remember that marriage is not a 50-50 deal. It takes 125 percent from both persons to ever get to the kind of understanding that will be required to keep going.

2

Try to put yourself in your mate's shoes. Instead of taking a position and then having to give up part of what you want for the sake of compromise, take time to figure out why you each want what you want and look for other ways to get it.

3

Learn to hold your tongue. I have never regretted *not* saying something, but I have certainly regretted some of the things I've said.

4

Don't forget to be a friend. Too often, we treat our significant others differently than we do our friends.

5

Try not to take things too personally. Instead, try to listen and understand what the other person means when he or she talks or behaves in certain ways.

6

Pay attention to the departures and reuniting with each other—not just when you're going to be away from each other for a long period, but the tender moments you can share on a routine daily basis, too.

7

Understand that no one person can be everything to another person. That's why it's so important to stay close to your girlfriends, even when the blush of young romance and demands of family, career, and life want to crowd them out. Life may seem full and complete now, but there will come a time when your women friends will sustain you.

8

Notice the things that your husband does right and tell him. Compliment him often and be specific so he'll know you're paying attention. He needs to hear it, especially from the one who means the most to him.

9

Try not to get into an argument with your spouse when you're hungry or tired—like right before dinner or at the end of a long day. Waiting to discuss something you know may be difficult to work through usually proves better.

10

One of the good things about being married is having someone to share all the little things of the day with, someone who cares what happened at work, and so forth. And the sharing needs to go both ways.

11

Don't go to bed angry. You almost always wake up happier if you have resolved the issue the night before.

12

Avoid the company of people who seem to be unhappy in their marriages, and watch and copy people who seem to be happy.

13

Laugh. Laugh at yourself and include each other in the joke. Try hard not to laugh at the other person unless they're trying to be funny.

14

Get a dog. They're funny and you'll always have something to focus on when other things are not very funny.

15

Pray daily for forgiveness and guidance.

16

Putting your partner first in almost everything, from serving the dinner plate to letting him have the remote, builds trust and strength in your relationship. You know he will be there for you and you for him.

Advice from Readers

Here is advice from readers of my column.

17

"Live each day so that at the end of it you have no regrets." My mother told me this is what she and Dad decided to do when they got married, and they were married for thirty years before my dad died of cancer.

—*Sue Slack*

18

It's not easy to give a new bride the secret to a long marriage in a few words. If the couple truly loves each other they have to realize first that divorce is never an option. The most important thing to realize is that love (passion) comes and goes. In the marriages that last, the couples ride out the hard, loveless times, and then one day, in a week, months, or many months, he'll walk in the door and your heart will skip a beat and you will find yourself falling in love all over again. I know that after thirty-nine years, many times I have asked myself why are we living together. We never talk, are caught up in work, children, just life; then I'll look at him and remember . . . and it starts all over again. As you grow older, the passion does leave; but the love gets stronger. Troubles come and go, children are born, time creeps up, and one day you look in the mirror and wonder how you became this old woman—no one else knows but the mate who has lived with you all these years. Can you imagine taking off your clothes for someone who didn't know how your body got this way?

—*Lucile Smith*

19

Learn to say that this or that is "ours," not "mine."

—*Gail Christopher*

20

Your spouse is your new family. Put some distance (maybe emotionally, physically, or both) between you and your parents and siblings. Whenever conflict arises, do not go running "home" to your parents. Learn to work things out together. You have a new home with your spouse. You two have to work as a team; sometimes it is not a fair distribution of responsibility, but that's marriage—work it out. Do not speak harshly about your spouse to your parents and siblings. Whenever you forgive your spouse, he or she may not be so quick to reciprocate, and this animosity may dampen everyone's relationship."

—*Heather Phillips*

21

Learn the difference between happiness and contentment. One is fleeting. The other will get you through difficult times. It's what helps you want what you have and accept what you're given with grace.

—*Valerie Gibbs*

22

Remember those precious words, "You are probably right . . ."

—*Dianne Gregory*

23

A good marriage requires love and respect, of

course, but also a healthy dose of humor, under-standing, and forgiveness.

—Sue McClure

24

Laugh. A lot. *With* each other and *at* each other. Hardly a day goes by that we don't laugh, usually good-naturedly, about something one of us has done or said. It keeps us grounded.

—Nancy and Mark Humphrey

25

Share. Share decision making. We rarely make a decision about making a donation or purchasing something for someone or for our home without running it by each other. It's not that we need the other's permission; it's just a considerate thing to do.

—Nancy and Mark Humphrey

26

Say "I love you" and say it often. I like hearing it as much as I like saying it.

—Nancy and Mark Humphrey

27

Even though couples tend to become more
alike the longer they are together, it's important
to remember to keep the individual traits that
attracted you to each other in the first place. It's
even better if you can keep the good traits and get
rid of the bad ones.

—Nancy and Mark Humphrey

28

Being thoughtful and considerate is crucial
to a marriage; perhaps it is even more important
to helping our children select loving, thoughtful
mates. Keith is incredibly patient and supportive
of me and our girls. Both girls have very clear

standards of what is required to build a stable relationship.

—*Rinnie Wood*

29

Do not correct your spouse in front of others. In most instances, whether something happened on the 3rd or 4th of the month really doesn't matter—so drop it. If it is really crucial, bring it up later and be sensitive in correcting. Something like, "I thought it was the 3rd, but was looking at my calendar and it was the 4th." Then laugh when you realize "how could we both have been wrong?"

—*Vicki Clark*

30

Always think about what you would want before you do or say anything. When my husband is a messy cook, I stop and think, "but he is cooking." Always, always, be grateful for who you have, remember the first day you knew you were in love, and never, ever, let yourself get in a situation that can lead to temptation. Respect always.

—*Wendy Mills*

31

I saw a list one time of ten things that can guarantee you a happy life. On that list, finding the right partner was #2, #4, and #7.

—*Tom Turnbull*

32

I've always heard about the three "C's"—compromise, commitment, and communication. But I have four "C's"—compromise, commitment, communication, and . . . cocktails!

—*Kathy West*

33

Patience, patience, patience. It's a lot of giving

and very little taking. But the main thing is whenever there is something you really, really want, make him think it was his idea.

—Meme Kriel

34

My husband and I have been married almost twenty-seven years. Several years ago we invented "Amnesty Statements," something that needed to be said but could possibly be construed as picking an argument with the other person. We use these sparingly and only when necessary, but they need to be said and heard without ill-feeling or rancor. Examples: "When your parents come to visit, I really need you to spend more time with them and not just leave me to entertain them," or, "When I come home from the grocery store I would like you to come help me unload the car, not just yell hello from in front of the TV." This works way better than what you may be thinking. It is just a statement of fact which is said simply to be heard and may (and often can) stop any feelings of anger or resentment. When one of us says, "I have an Amnesty Statement," the other one knows to stop and listen, that it is important.

—*Abby Kropp*

35

Make kindness, gentleness, and courtesy the norm in your home every day. As has been said by another, "Treat your family like guests and your guests like family."

—*Sandra Lackey*

36

Set up shared time, equal for all holidays, from the beginning.

—*Gail Christopher*

37

The first rule of love is to listen, an anonymous saying on a magnet on our fridge. Never assume you know all about each other, but keep on listening to each other for all your lives. Focus on each other with heart and mind and ears and eyes.

—*Johnnie Godwin*

38

Never miss the opportunity to compliment your spouse in the company of others. Everyone likes to be praised, and by sincerely complimenting your sweetheart in front of others, he feels appreciated doubly. Even if he is only in earshot, he'll hear you!

—*Anita Bell*

39

When my husband and I got back from our honeymoon, our church was having a marriage seminar. The best thing that ever happened was the suggestion there that you pray for your spouse—Lord, make him (or her) the man (or woman) that you would have him to be and give me the grace to live with him. This puts everything into the right perspective when your spouse isn't doing what "you" think that he should be doing—that is, taking out the trash, helping with housework, and so forth. You trust that God is working in him and through him and you don't have to nag to get him to become who you want him to be. Of course, you would rather have him become who God wants more than who you want him to be. This is only for couples who truly believe that God is shaping their lives together, but it has worked for us for twenty-five years and I expect it will for many years to come!

—*Bea Andrew*

40

Don't give up all your independence! While you do want to share many interests and show your love and caring for your spouse and his or her activities, keep—or develop—some of your own unique pursuits. You don't want to be totally co-dependent on your spouse for your identity and self-worth. Remember, your spouse found you to be an interesting person when you were single, and you want that to continue—for his or her sake and your own!

—*Bea Leff*

41

Whenever I am nitpicky and critical of every little thing my husband does, I try to think about the things he puts up with from me. Just about every time, I realize that I came out on the good end of this deal called marriage. I heard this one time and it helps on those days when you wonder, *Who is this person I am married to?* Think back and remember the things that attracted you to your spouse in the beginning. Sure we change over the years (a lot), but by recalling those things, sometimes that light comes on and you see them in a new way. It also helps to appreciate some of those changes that have taken place. Look at how far you both have come and appreciate what you have right now.

—*Beverly Tidwell*

42

I believe one of the best things (a new couple) can do for each other is to buy the CD by Gary Chapman *The Five Love Languages,* and carefully listen to it together. The five languages are:

- Touch
- Words of affirmation
- Quality time
- Acts of service
- Gifts

Listening to the CD helps each partner to identify the importance he or she attaches to each one. Often that thing (language) one attempts to give the other is the one that the giver most wants for himself, but it may not be the one the mate most values. The giver may then begin to feel that his loving efforts are not appreciated. Learning the order of importance one's spouse attaches to the five languages is, in a way, learning the emotional language of the other. My wife of twenty-six years and I learned a lot from listening to Chapman. I am certain it would help newlyweds begin to understand each other and the other's needs.

Learning early in the marriage will bring, and keep, husband and wife closer together.

—*Bill Gaskill*

43

Here's advice that I still try to remember after twenty-three years of being happily married: When you have those days or times when you just can't stand him, or those days when she is completely on your nerves (those days will come), remind yourself why you married your spouse in the first place . . . is he kind and thoughtful, good to his family, is she strong in her faith, does he make you laugh, and so forth. It will usually put a smile back on your face and help you be more grateful.

—*Anonymous*

44

I, as the husband, would like to ask that the lucky groom not take his wife for granted. Treat her like you were still trying to convince her to marry you. Yes, I still open the car door for my wife. Kiss your wife at least every morning and evening. Never go to bed with disagreements not settled.

—*Clayton Hicks*

45

I've been happily married for seven years and one thing that has really been great for my husband and me is finding hobbies we both enjoy. Even though most couples are very different, if you try hard enough, you can definitely find something you both love. My husband and I have gone through many stages of things we enjoy together, such as hiking, traveling, camping, and so on. Most of our hobbies are free or very cheap, which makes it more fun for us because it doesn't add the stress of a financial burden. We even cut coupons and go through the Sunday paper together . . . and this is a hobby for us! I've found that even on days when we may not be "madly in love" with each other, if we get out and do something fun together, I am reminded that he is my best friend.

—*Tressa Gibbs*

46

Over the years I've read from many so-called authorities that both parties should always speak what's on their minds—"to clear the air," if you will. I'm sorry, but that is wrong, wrong, *wrong* and has probably resulted in countless divorces. In my case, I have a very high temper that through the years I learned to control, both at work, around friends—and certainly at home. Although it sounds trite, it does indeed take two to make an argument. If I ever jumped in with both feet to take up "my side" of an argument when an issue was raised by my wife, I would have been divorced many times over. With the high temper I have, words would have flown that could never be taken back and would never be forgiven.

So my advice to young people *(who will never heed this),* is to simply clam up when your spouse happens to begin a tirade. Just don't say *any-*

thing. Zip it! This too shall pass. The anger will pass—yours and your spouse's—but if allowed to develop into a full-fledged, bitter argument, the effects will linger long after it is over. Plain and simple, if you love your spouse, it's worth biting your tongue until it all blows over.

Don't get me wrong. I'm *not* saying change your personality, and give in to every single thing that pops up in your marriage, allowing yourself to be pushed around by your spouse. I'm speaking only about serious arguments that you can see escalating. And trust me, we can all see them when it's happening.

Many wiser than I am will strongly disagree and it might not work for everyone. But it worked for *me*—through more than fifty years of marriage.

—*A happy man over the years*

47

Remember what is important and don't get caught up in things that aren't. Too many of my generation's marriages fell to the stress of attaining dream houses or producing super-achieving children.

—Nina Fortmeyer

48

Always be aware of the things that make you a difficult person to be married to! I wake up every day, grateful that my husband puts up with me, and I think he feels the same way about me. It's made for fifteen very happy years together.

—Becky

49

Make sure *before* you tie the knot that you can live with all the little irritating things that you don't like about your future spouse. These are things that probably will not change unless that person chooses to make the change. Don't fall into the trap of believing your future mate will change for you after you are married. It usually does not happen. Even God won't change a person unless that person allows Him to.

—*Brenda Allen*

50

Don't play the "I-make-more-than-you-game." In our marriage we are *thrilled* when one of us gets a raise or a bonus because that's more money for Team Solomon.

—*Cindy Solomon*

51

I've been happily married twenty-one years. Believe your husband is better than he really is by speaking words of encouragement rather than criticism. Those positive seeds you are planting will reap the man you want him to be because he will want to live up to your expectations. This is true for children too.

—*Buffie Baril*

52

Don't set any precedents you don't intend
to keep, such as foot massages, cooking dinner,
mowing the grass, raking leaves, driving the kids
to school, and so forth. Ha ha!

—Sharon Pigott

53

I think everyone, in that first blush of romance,
thinks the good times will last forever. Young
couples should expect and be prepared for some
bad times, whether it is health issues, money
problems, issues with children, or whatever. This
doesn't mean that they should be pessimistic,
but they should be realistic, and above all else to
remember that this too will pass.

Bad times don't last any more than good
times do. Life is a series of ups and downs. Work
through them both together as a team. So many
young people give up at the first crisis and end up
divorced. See the bad times as an opportunity for
growth as a team. When you get older and look
back over the years, you'll really love each other

even more for how you worked together and supported each other.

—Anita Bell

54

Never criticize your in-laws to your significant other. Make friends with your in-laws and stay friends with them. But set your limits before the children come along.

—Gail Christopher

55

Always remember to laugh—together, often, and with friends.

—Elise McMillan

56

We agreed to stay out of debt as much as possible, buying only a house and car on credit and even then buying only in the price range that we could afford. Today, we pay cash for our car or we wait until we can afford one. We have paid off two houses in our sixty years of marriage. We pooled our financial resources and never bought expensive items without prior consent from the other. We did not think that it was necessary to have all the things that our parents had accumulated over a lifetime in the first year of our marriage. We took it one thing at a time.

—*Clayton Hicks*

57

Always remember your manners. And think before you speak.

—*Linda Tyree*

58

The best advice I was given from my mother was never to go to bed mad. I have not always met this goal, but it is certainly worth aspiring to.

—*Christy Lyons*

59

When you fight, you must not be cruel.

—Ann Manning

60

Don't talk about politics after you've had two cocktails.

—Gail and Les Kerr

61

Give the person who just came home time to breathe.

—Gail and Les Kerr

62

Help one another, always.

—Gail and Les Kerr

63

The harder it is, the more you *must* talk about it.

—*Gail and Les Kerr*

64

It is not required that you like all the same things. In fact, that would be boring.

—*Gail and Les Kerr*

65

Your spouse is not going to change. So love them the way they are, and work on changing how you deal with stuff they do that bugs you.

—*Gail and Les Kerr*

66

At parties, split up. But have a super-secret signal to use when either one is ready to leave.

—*Gail and Les Kerr*

67

Marry the right person in the first place!

—*Gail and Les Kerr*

68

Communicating is vital to a successful marriage, but the choices of *how* and *when* one communicates are even more important.

—*Rinnie Wood*

69

I would have to say that some great advice would be not to forget to use "common courtesy." Always say "please" and "thank you." This will keep your husband from thinking that he is being taken for granted. It makes your wife feel appreciated.

—*Bet Baswell*

70

It's not the time you spend apart that matters, but what you do with your time together. We are all unique in our needs and desires. Know what it takes to make yourself feel loved and your spouse to feel loved, and do whatever it takes to make that happen.

—*Carol Wiek*

71

I can certainly speak to how to have a long marriage: It's easy—no matter what happens, don't get divorced. I know that sounds flippant, but I am dead serious. How to live happily ever after is far more difficult. Is any marriage happy all the time? I seriously doubt it. To expect it to be is unrealistic. The tricky part of being happy is to quickly forgive the offenses and to focus on the good things. Over the forty-seven years that we've been married, I have learned:

- That the best gift you can give your children is a happy marriage. It requires that you keep your priorities straight: your spouse-marriage comes first—before children, before anybody else or anything else.

- To be clear about who the most important person in your life is, then treat that person as the special person he or she is.
- To keep marital troubles within the marriage. Do not hesitate to see a therapist or counselor if you get stuck. They can be incredibly helpful, whereas consulting family members or friends is not.
- To know that a good marriage is a 50-50 proposition and always be willing to do more than your share.
- To focus on the family unit. Do things together as a family. Be conscious of making memories for your children to cherish.
- That respect is critical to any meaningful relationship. Love and respect are elements that must be maintained. Work at it. It is worth it.
- That there are elements of contentedness and accomplishment that weathering storms

together provide. Don't give up the ship.
• Being happy is a choice.

—Barbara Speight

72

More than anything else, I believe our commitment from the beginning that marriage is a lifelong journey has helped us through the tough times. Every marriage will face times when there are frustrations with circumstance, your partner, or both that will challenge you to give up. In these times, the awareness that this covenant is for always will not only sustain you, it will keep you happy.

—Charles Lott

73

Be nice to each other's friends—especially the closest ones. Your spouse probably knew them before marrying you and values the friendships. Recognize that sometimes your spouse needs to

maintain a friendship and its O.K. to encourage
and support that. The result will be reciprocal.

—Dinah Tysinger

74

Don't hold grudges. Talk (communicate) and
let the little things go.

—Sandra Lackey

75

Everyone always comments about the importance of sexual fidelity in marriage, but there is
another area of equal importance, in my opinion.
That is the business partnership that a marriage
is. Every young couple should decide together
upon the standard of living they expect to achieve
(not what they dream is possible), and what it will
take from both of them to reach that goal. One
person is usually better at handling the money
and the day-to-day task of paying the bills, but
large items regarding security in the future, the

purchase of a home, and children are definitely topics that should be discussed before marriage and decided upon as a couple. If the sex is bad there may be a cure, but if the finances are bad, chances are that a marriage may end in divorce, because fretting about money colors everything else in life.

—Cheryl Lavender

76

Keep the flame of romance alive by doing the little things. I thank my husband every day for the small things that he does (making me a cup of coffee, folding the laundry). And he thanks me for what I do. It really makes you feel appreciated. And when you feel appreciated you will want to do whatever it takes to make the other person happy, not because you have to, but because you want to.

—Brenda Allen

77

Married forty-four years: Be honest with each other and don't agree just to keep from having an argument, only later to resent your spouse because you conceded. Honesty is the best policy.

—*Gerrie McMahan*

78

Don't keep separate banking accounts. I know that some people have to keep separate expense accounts for business purposes, but finances in our marriage have always been a team effort with one checking account, one savings account, one emergency fund, and IRA's and other retirement investments in both our names.

—*Cindy Solomon*

79

The three most important words in marriage are *"You are right!"*

—*Virginia Holladay*

80

My wonderful husband and I have been married for more than sixty-two happy years, happy most of the time. My good friend's mother gave me this advice: "Never get mad at the same time." I think that was the best advice, and I have practiced this for all these years. It has kept me from doing things that I would be sorry for forever.

—*Margaret Giles*

81

Honor and respect your mate's parents. They are a big part of who your mate is today. The old mother-in-law jokes go both ways. Your mom-in-law can be just as intimidated by you as you are of her. Give them the benefit of the doubt. Parents always think of their children as their special gifts to the world and just want to be part of their lives. Also, they have a lot of wisdom that can be tapped into if you just try to see it. Parents of married children just want to feel a little bit needed even though their kids are "all grown up." I never thought I would miss my in-laws as much as I do now that they are gone from my life. I still had so much to learn from them. We all have an endless amount of love to share—be generous with that love.

—*Claudette Walsh*

82

Laugh as much as possible, keep good friends close by, and don't sweat the small stuff.

—*Janice Guthrie*

83

My wife and I agreed early in our marriage that it was O.K. to disagree as long as we did not do verbal abuse or tissue damage. Don't go back to Mama or Daddy just because you have an argument. Settle it as two mature adults. We also think that praying together and attending church on a regular basis has been a strong plus for us.

—*Clayton Hicks*

84

There is a Bible verse, Philippians 2:3, that says, "Let nothing be done through selfish ambition or conceit, but in lowliness of mind let each esteem others better than himself." This goes completely against our human nature, but I have found it to be some of the best advice in dealing not only with my husband, but with children and everyone else for that matter. It's not saying that you should let people run over you or hurt you. It's about the condition of your own heart and being humble enough to let their happiness and well-being be of the utmost importance to you. It's not easy to have a servant's heart, but it is well worth cultivating. This doesn't always work out for the best with your children, though, because they will *run all over you!* Just remember that your spouse will be there long after your children have moved on.

—*Beverly Tidwell*

85

Set goals together at the beginning of each new year. The goals should be for financial, spiritual, and relational areas of your lives. This way you know you are a team going in the same direction with a vision in sight of what you want. If you write your goals on paper, you can refer to them when the need arises and remember what is important.

—Charity Kimes

86

Don't take advice from people just because they have been married thirty-plus years. Make sure they have been "happily" married for thirty-plus years. I've seen people who have been married for many years who can't seem to stand being in the same room together.

—Brenda Allen

87

The pastor who married my husband and me

more than ten years ago gave this advice for a long, happy marriage: "Just choose to stay and make it work. Marriage is tough and rocky, but being committed to making it work is the key. We all have a million different reasons that we could walk away, but we have to choose to stay." Obviously, there are situations where people need to get out. Life is complicated. But this advice has worked really well for us and all that we've been through—raising kids has rocked our world!

—*Mary Chandler*

88

Small gestures of love keep a long relationship from going stale. When I came home from my first day of teaching after being at home raising children for a long time, I wearily plodded into the bathroom to wash up. There I found roses, a gin and tonic, and a tub full of warm water and bubble bath! Don had sneaked home earlier in the day and set all that up.

—*Teddie Clark*

89

After thirty-five years of married life we attribute our happiness and success to the following: A strong sense of humor between each other, candid discussions, and a sincere reliance on prayer for good times and not so good times. This is our formula for happiness.

—Barry and Kathy Cullen

90

My dad told me on the day of my wedding never to go in a place that you wouldn't take your wife. We have been married for fifty-one years.

—David Gibbs

91

Talk, talk, talk. If your decisions are made together, there will be more tolerance when things don't go as planned. When purchases are made in agreement, the weight of "debt" is easier to bear. Begin your day asking what each can do for the other—sometimes it's help with a chore, sometimes it's a "frivolous" desire, sometimes it's just an extra touch. After thirty-nine years of sharing coffee with my favorite coffee "mate," I still learn new things about my husband every single day!

—*Dennis and Jolaine Thomas*

92

Always take the time to listen to your lifelong partner, even if it is during the time that you are watching television. A lot of times, what your spouse is saying is more important than television.

—*Anonymous*

93

Don't flatulate in the marital bed. The bedroom should be a place that's peaceful and serene. Unpleasant fumes take away from the romance and the desire to be close to each other. Set the stage by resisting the urge and going to the rest-

room when you have gas. Your spouse will greatly appreciate it.

—Dinah Tysinger

94

Don't pick an argument when you know you
are PMSing. When little things start to irritate
me, I have only to look at the calendar to see that
it's the week before I start my period. Those are
the times that I really bite my tongue, because on
ordinary days those same things would not
affect me.

—Brenda Allen

95

Married sixty-one years: I think that learning
to ask for help with a task, as opposed to waiting for your husband to see the need himself, can
save a lot of frustration. I found that if I asked
Paul to empty the trash when it needed emptying,
instead of waiting for him to notice (and getting

irritated that he had not taken it out) it made for a better day!

—*Corinne Wilson*

96

Just treat your spouse as well as you treat your dog.

—*Donald Barnett*

97

Thinking back the last forty-nine years, I know that what has been most significant in having a contented marriage and being partners, is helping each other from the start. Not too much but just being intuitive to know how and when to help your partner. Remember it is not a "gender thing," like his job (role) or her job (role). Just do what it takes to help get the job done together.

—*Dottie Caul*

98

I try to find *something* to praise him for or
thank him for every day, like, "Thank you for
folding the laundry," or "Wow, the grass looks
great since you cut it."

—*Mary Herbert Kelly*

99

After forty-three years of marriage, the best
advice I can give anyone is to keep your differences with your spouse *private.* Do not berate or
embarrass your mate in front of family or friends.
Example: When my husband and I were first married, my husband wanted to go on a fishing trip
with his buddies. It just happened to be several
days before payday. I knew that, until his pay-
check came in, we did not have the funds for him
to go. I made the mistake of bringing this matter
to his attention in front of his friends. My husband was embarrassed and then furious! He told
me later that I could tell him *anything* but please
do it in private. The problem was magnified by
bringing friends into the situation. The same goes

for bringing family into little tiffs. Although you and your spouse will get over the situation quickly, the opinions of your spouse held by family members can be tainted by tales of bad behavior that are colored by the heat of the moment in your telling all to them.

—*Joanne Wilson*

100

Problems arise in all marriages. Some are easy enough for couples to work out on their own, but others require the help of an objective outsider who has had formal training in counseling, unlike the couple's friends and family usually have. Couples should try to recognize those problems that are beyond their skill set to solve on their own, and they should see no shame or disgrace in asking for professional help in solving those problems. The sooner a couple struggling with a problem seeks help, the greater the couple's chances are of weathering the storm with the marriage intact. I liken counseling and therapy to furniture movers. There are times in life when you're put in the position of having to move a grand piano from one room to another. This is a massive piece of furniture that one person simply cannot shift all alone, though many a person tries and ends up hurting himself and many things around him. A smart person who needs to move a piano calls a moving company with experience in relocating pianos and other heavy furniture. These movers have been trained to do it correctly, without hurting themselves or the rest of the house. Counselors help us move the grand pianos in our lives. It's very silly for us to try to do it by ourselves or with our friends (who don't know how to move pianos safely) when there is plenty of good, trained help out there.

—*Elizabeth Lindsey*

101

Always give each other some "down" time at the end of the day. Whether it is five minutes or fifteen, don't bombard each other as soon as you get in the door. Typically there is still some tension left from whatever went on at work, and you don't want to accidentally take that out on each other. Spend time with your dog, change clothes, go for a short walk—whatever works best.

—*Emily Day*

102

Put the work into your marriage while it's fun. In other words, date and talk and play together now. It's much easier to make those things a priority than to have to put work into counseling and damage repair in the future.

—*Becky*

103

Know that it's all right to disagree, but that disagreement doesn't have to be mean-spirited or hurtful—it can be done with love. Enjoy your differences as well as what you have in common.

—*Gary Keplinger*

104

Even if you share finances, say "thank you" for dinner at the end of a meal. It's nice to maintain the polite manners you enjoyed while dating. Don't forget the chivalry. It takes thought and effort and goes a long way. Always kiss each other good night. Happy husband, Happy life, Happy wife, Happy life.

—Dinah Tysinger

105

Married forty-four years: Give each other space. Let your spouse hang out with his friends and family and you do the same. But make sure you check in before making any plans with your friends or family. Your spouse should do the same. That way, there are no hard feelings of being left out, or of making plans when your spouse wants to do something with you.

—Gerrie McMahan

106

As time passes, you either grow together or you grow apart; nothing stays the same. The ticket is to grow together.

—Beverley and Dick Grabenkort

107

Resolve to always work things out—never give up on your commitment to each other.

—Beverley and Dick Grabenkort

108

Communication—that's huge. No secrets.

—Beverley and Dick Grabenkort

109

Earn absolute trust and never, ever do anything to betray it. With that trust comes freedom and security, which create a safe haven for each of you.

—Beverley and Dick Grabenkort

110

Each of us has an area of weakness or sensitivity, and when there is an argument you must resolve never to go after your mate's weakness.

—Beverley and Dick Grabenkort

111

Learn to enjoy small moments—it's so easy, especially in the early years when life is so hectic, to lose that ability. Try to focus on the moment.

—Beverley and Dick Grabenkort

112

Do unexpected things to please your mate.

—Beverley and Dick Grabenkort

113

Say you're sorry.

—Beverley and Dick Grabenkort

114

Give; give more; think of the other person; give it up—you don't have to win at the other's expense; get the ego out of the relationship.

—*Beverley and Dick Grabenkort*

115

Treasure each other.

—*Beverley and Dick Grabenkort*

116

We enter into marriage with numerous expectations. After a few years, we realize the results either fell short of those expectations or did not even resemble what we expected. Try to keep your expectations in check.

—*Heather Phillips*

117

I think one of the keys to maintaining a long

and happy marriage is directly expressing your appreciation and love for your partner on a daily basis. I think that we are good at doing that at first, but over time, we tend to think about and comment only on what someone is doing wrong, not what they are doing right. I think partners in marriage get frustrated when they feel like what they are contributing is underappreciated or not appreciated at all. This, over time, can lead some married individuals to seek appreciation and affection in others, who see them from a fresh light and give them compliments, and this can lead to marital distress and even infidelity.

—Joe Henske

118

My husband and I have been married for thirty-six years. I feel like the most important thing that keeps our marriage happy and long-lasting is our faith in God. We made a commitment to each other to love each other and put each other first in our lives through the good and the bad, and we made this commitment before God. Prayer for understanding and forgiveness and guidance is important in a marriage as well. Remember, you loved your mate so much in the beginning that you made this commitment, so don't ever let anyone or anything come between what God joined together. The years go by quickly, and the security and love in a happy marriage are priceless. I'd marry my guy all over again. I love him more today than I did the day I married him.

—*Julie Ann Smith*

119

The trick to keeping the "flame hot" in a marriage is to date! Yes, I actually said *date;* however, date the person you married! We have "date night" every couple of weeks. Too many couples forget to look nice for each other and end up watching TV weekend after weekend. No wonder people go out looking for action! Here are a few examples of our "date nights" (without the ending!). First, dress up as though you are actually going out with someone you want to impress! Our stay-at-home date: we plan a menu where we both participate in preparing the food—sometimes it is all appetizers served at our bar. We get dressed up, turn on music, light candles, dance and converse, and have a great dinner. Our date out: one person is in charge of planning and inviting. We have sent an invitation in the mail, put it in a briefcase, hidden it under a pillow, or taped it to the mirror. Our other key is to exercise together, which we have also done for all these years. P.S. We have been happily married thirty-six years.

—*Jane Gregg*

120

Feed him well, give him plenty of sex, and don't bitch at him. It sounds pretty simple, because it is. A friend asked once, "That's great for him, but what do you get out of it?" I quickly replied, "Anything I want!"

—*Melinda Bacurin*

121

There was this great column in *USA Weekend*

the year my husband and I married. It was titled "Choice Is the Heart of a Marriage," from NPR's This I Believe series. I always share the gist of the column with my engaged girlfriends and I wanted to share it with you. "I believe that love is embedded in the sacred of the ordinary—of love communicated each time he cooks oatmeal and I schedule his dental appointment. In the contented, peaceful silence of our predictable, boring day, I choose him all over again."

—Jennifer Hill

122

"I haven't been married that long—six and a half years—but I've been married long enough to have learned a few things. One thing that I would advise (newly married people) is to avoid the temptation to badmouth each other in public. And by "public," I don't just mean the people you see each day. I also mean Twitter, Facebook, MySpace, blogs, and other open Internet formats. It's so easy to send out a tweet with a snarky put-down of your spouse or write an angry blog post in the heat of the moment. But it's not so easy to take those words back once they're out there in cyberspace. Lots of people may get and keep the wrong impression of you, your spouse, and your marriage. You and your spouse will likely kiss and make up, but there might be a whole lot of people out there whose impression of you, your spouse, and your marriage will rest with a sarcastic tweet on Twitter or a frustrated note on Facebook. And who needs that? Does that mean you can never gently poke fun at your spouse? No, of course not. But think before you tweet, post, or blog. Think about whom you're most loyal to. Think about whom you made those promises to when you got married.

—*Jennifer Larson*

123

Choose your battles! Decide if it is worth your marriage for him to pick his socks up off the living room floor or for the dishes to be done when *you* think they should be. Although there are many times these day-to-day things can be frustrating, decide if it is *that* battlefield on which you want to sacrifice a portion of your happiness. If not, then wait until something important and worth fighting for comes along. You will find your spouse much more receptive to the important details if there are fewer skirmishes over the minutiae.

—Jennifer Radcliffe

124

We married the day before Pearl Harbor, December 6, 1941. The day we married, Jim freed me to be myself. I'm not sure I was that wise, but I learned it really isn't possible to change anyone but yourself. We both must have known that from the get-go. Now in our nineties, we really celebrate every day!

—Keyes Tate

125

Commitment is the glue that binds two people together in a marriage, through good and bad, sickness and health, for better or worse, just like the vow states. Commitment.

—Judy Anderson

126

Know that marriages often grow like trees whose greatest strengths may be where they were wounded but have grown over and around the wounds. Try to split a log where it was wounded and produced a knot. That's where the tree is the hardest. Marriage may be similar.

—Johnnie Godwin

127

Don't feel like you have to do everything together. I love to shop and garden, and Robin loves to go to Friday night football games and car shows. Although neither of us lets these separate pursuits get in the way of our overall relationship, I don't begrudge Robin if he goes out one Friday night to see a football game. Likewise, he graciously let me attend Master Gardener classes at night a few years ago. Some time apart makes the time together sweeter. But we also make time for date nights. This seems like a no-brainer when you're first married, but life can get complicated when you add children, careers, a home, pets, hobbies, and extended family into the mix. I am a natural planner, so I schedule things just for us to do (with Robin's input and O.K. of course) at least once or twice a month. Sometimes we play golf at a local public course or go hiking; other times we go out for dinner or catch a play. It really doesn't matter what you do so long as you both enjoy it and it's just the two of you.

—*Cindy Solomon*

128

Do not keep separate accounts. Never reimburse each other for things. Don't have "her" possessions and "his" possessions. Once you're married you need to understand that everything you have and everything with which you struggle or celebrate is yours equally. Even if you don't have children yet or if you never will, by choice

or by circumstance, you are already a family of
two and must treat each other that way.

—*Judy Feaster*

129

Communication is the key. Sometimes it is
difficult to have a conversation with kids or life
happening around us. We make sure we have at
least one date a month to talk and keep our marriage sacred. We go out to have dinner or simply
get coffee at a local place. This allows us to talk
without interruption and enjoy each other's company. If we stay at home and don't make a special effort to get a babysitter, we find ourselves
in the regular tasks of home life. We always say
we would rather spend money on dinner together
than pay for a marriage counselor. It works!

—*Karen Hande*

130

Pick your battles. In my first marriage, I
nagged and criticized everything about my hus-

band that was not in line with what I would do. I thought that I could teach him the way to do things right. It made for a very unhappy situation. My second marriage is much better, because I "don't sweat the small stuff." Picking up underwear is now second nature to me, while the important things get some "counseling sessions" in our living room. Try not to worry about every little thing.

—*Karen Malone*

131

My dear grandparents were married sixty-seven years. They always said that mutual respect for each other was the key to a happy marriage.

—*Karen Richards*

132

Build memories. Memories are the story of you as a couple. A story that is true only for the two of you. When the wedding gifts are old and used, when the children have come and gone, the memories are your shared history—the story of how you've lived as a couple. Build them intentionally, build them carefully—they are priceless.

—*Karen Kendrick*

133

Remember you are a team. Do not speak badly of each other to friends or family out of anger. When you are out together, always have each other's back.

—*Kristin Garrett*

134

Pillow Talk. Yes, pillow talk has saved many marriages. Lying there in the dark quiet, no phones, no TV, no kids, no touching, just you and your partner lying in the dark talking about your day, your thoughts, and planning your tomorrows and really saying "I love you" and meaning it and hearing it. Pillow talk—how easy is that?

—*Linda Carter*

135

Avoid the "how does my hair look" question when she gets home from the beauty shop. Comments like "that hairdresser's license should be revoked" are not likely to yield good results. I personally prefer the "lie like a dog" approach, with comments like "that hairdresser deserves an extra tip as that was the best haircut I have ever seen."

—*Lee Hayslip*

136

Make time for each other. Life will only get busier with work, travel, kids, pets, friends, all sorts of things. As the years pass and the new of newlywed wears off, it's important to set aside time to be together. And it doesn't matter what you do: double-date with friends or even your parents; surprise your spouse with a night away; pick up take-out and eat on your back porch; go for a picnic; save up for a fancy dinner to celebrate a special occasion. Making time for dates demonstrates how much you value each other and your relationship.

—*Leslie and David Hudson*

137

My advice for the newlyweds would be never to include family members (especially mothers and mothers-in-law) in any argument or fight that you might have. When the couple has "kissed and made up" and forgotten about the whole thing, family members tend to hold a grudge and may still be upset with the spouse.

—*Lisa Johnson*

138

Send your spouse a card every month that best reflects how you feel. On the inside, write something relevant to the previous month—either poignant, funny, remorseful, sweet—or anything from the heart.

—*John Malone*

139

We have two phrases that we often use: Ironically, they have to do with the same topic: Owning up to your mistakes. The first phrase is, "You are right, I did do or say that and I am sorry." This one is a winner if your spouse confronts you for harming him in some way. The second phrase is, "Can I make a repair attempt?" This one works really well if you use it the second you realize you have done or said something hurtful. It is hard to stay mad at someone when he comes and owns up for something he has done by saying that. It is a fact that arguments and disagreements are going to happen, but learning how to deal with them and accepting and admitting your part in things goes a long way. We have been married for sixteen years, and we have been together for twenty-two.

—*Lisa and Marty Quinn*

140

My two cents would be Ephesians 4:26: "Do not let the sun go down on your wrath."

—*Marty Chapman*

141

Keep these two quotations tucked in your mind: "Never forget that the goodness you see in your spouse is God's gift to you, a touch of his grace" (John Bosio, *Tennessee Register,* May 20, 2005). And, "For two people in a marriage to live together day after day is unquestionably the one miracle the Vatican has overlooked" (Bill Cosby). Last, after being married fifteen years, my husband and I love the book *101 Nights of Grrreat Romance,* by Laura Corn.

—*Mary Beth Scango*

142

Although marriage is a partnership, it's hardly ever a 50/50 proposition. At times, it can be 60/40, 80/20, or even 90/10. It takes dedication during difficult times, believing that the marriage will be stronger having gone through them together. Another very important tip: never under any circumstances should you approach your husband during a football game (especially the

Titans) and say, "Honey, we need to talk."

—*Melissa*

143

Marriage is a life commitment that is most successful if based on a living friendship between mates. Just like a biological family and close friends, there will be times, maybe years, when you don't like each other. But keeping your relationship is more important than being right, so be watchful of pride. The love you have for each other will always be there even if you sometimes don't want to admit it. Over the years, life, work, and children happen, so it's easy to lose touch. Make a point of having private, quiet time together every week and take vacations without kids every year. As you each change through life, you'll be a part of each other's change. Most important for me is that my wife is my best friend and is the only person I let into my most emotional, intimate space. Always remember the love you have for each other. Even "God is love."

—*Mark Russell*

144

If both have been working before getting married, then both have learned to live on one income. Continue to live on one income after you get married and use the other person's income as a bonus. Use it to pay off your mortgage if one of you owns a house, save for a house if renting, save for a new car, save for a big vacation, and so forth. Since many problems in marriages relate to finances, I feel this will greatly reduce disagreements about finances. It will also relieve stress related to the chance of one spouse losing a job, because the couple will be able to continue living as before, just without the extra saving.

—*Jamie Meyer*

145

Unselfishness. Commitment. And communication. Be committed to each other and communicate openly and often.

—*Laura Riley*

146

If you must fight—fight fair. Don't ever resort to name-calling. These are words that you can truly never "take back." Once they are out there they will most likely always be in the back of the recipient's head even if followed by sorry, hugs, and kisses. My five sisters gave me this advice when I got married nine years ago, and as I have found out, it's so important to keep your marriage above this level.

—*Michelle West*

147

No one is perfect, so pick your battles. Stand by your argument only if it's really important to you. If it's not that important, then let it go and let him win.

—*Monserrate Santiago*

148

Once children come along, *always* make sure they know that your relationship (the marriage) is paramount as far as earthly relationships are concerned. Children need the security of knowing that their parents love each other and are committed to a lifelong relationship, and they need to see behaviors and hear statements that validate that. Go so far as to refuse to allow them to disrespect your spouse—just the same way you would defend your spouse against disrespect from someone outside the family.

—Rob Mossack

149

Find a couple whose marriage you admire and ask them if they will walk through at least one full year of everyday life with you. Meet as you need, but at least once per month for a "check-in." During this "check-in" time, agree in advance to discuss real topics—chores, finances, communication, intimacy, and so forth. Of course, not all of those at one time! Time with the mentor couple is not a counseling session. The older couple listens mostly and shares what worked for them. There is great healing power in knowing you are not the only one to have ever struggled with a particular issue.

—*Nancy Bowron*

150

My best advice for a happy marriage is to give your partner time to think things over. I have learned that topics that start with "I would like for you to think about. . ." or "when you get time, give some thought to. . ." have a far greater chance of cooperation than the ones that start with "I want to. . ." or "we have to . . ." Snap judgments can lead to "no way" or arguments.

—*Naomi Hughes*

151

Be yourselves and love each other. The other stuff is just stuff. Shortly after I got married, my father sent me a letter with his observations on marriage, which I paraphrased and passed on to many of my friends as they got married. It deals more with conflict than my own advice, because my parents are very different from each other. They have been married fifty-four years and are very much in love. I pass on "Arnold's Rules of Marriage."

1. A marriage is not a war, with the result that no one ever won. If either of you try to dominate the other, even if you appear to succeed, you will not have won. The marriage will have lost, though.

2. The husband is not the wife's dad and the wife is not his mother. The sooner you both forget what a husband or wife is "supposed to do," the happier you will be.

3. This stems from a Chinese proverb: "Just because you have silenced an opponent does not mean that you have convinced him." When you disagree, talk it out. Shouting may be good for the ego, but it leaves scars on the marriage. It also leaves the question unresolved.

4. Never start a sentence with "you always," "you never," or "you should."

5. Don't bring outsiders into your disagreements. Once someone else is involved, it

becomes harder to compromise without losing face.

6. Don't let an argument fester. Talk it out before it becomes a permanent part of your lives.

—*Nina Fortmeyer*

152

The best marital advice that I can give is something that my husband and I live by. I wake up every morning and think about something I can do to make my husband happy for that day. I believe he does the same for me, and if both spouses try to follow this tactic, then the marriage will be a happy and successful one.

—*Brett Scher*

153

Honor and respect your husband. Do not complain about him or be gossipy about him to friends. If you are unhappy, talk to him about it.

—*Tiffany Foss*

154

Don't question your spouse's decisions in front of others. If you have questions about a decision, wait until you're alone to discuss it.

—Tiffany Foss

155

Do not be afraid to get help. If you're stuck, don't be ashamed to seek counsel from a pastor or other professional. Usually they can offer tools to help you and your spouse communicate better.

—Tiffany Foss

156

Listen to your spouse, affirm them in the things that they're passionate about.

—Tiffany Foss

157

Don't get too busy. With children, work, and

activities, it's easy to get too busy. Take time out for date nights just with each other.

—*Tiffany Foss*

158

Spouse first, children second—though this is sure hard sometimes!

—*Tiffany Foss*

159

Make each other laugh.

—*Tiffany Foss*

160

Always be honest, no secrets—ever, even if it's about how much you paid for those shoes, or that you even bought them.

—*Tiffany Foss*

161

Consider yourself his biggest ally.

—Tiffany Foss

162

It's easy to write these things, but I always pray that I can live them out every day. Some are easier than others.

—Tiffany Foss

163

I have a shirt that says, "In life, the little things are the big things." That's my and my husband's philosophy on marriage. It's not the fancy dinners out or the expensive gifts that mean the most, it's the home-cooked meals, the handmade gifts from the kids, the hand-picked flowers. If you remember the small things, married life is wonderful!

—Melanie Williams

164

In everything you do, treat your spouse with respect. This also works for your children and everyone else you meet.

—*Bob Nadler*

165

You (this goes for each spouse) don't really have a life to share with another person unless you have taken the responsibility of providing your own happiness, character, and purpose.

—*Sally Hughes*

166

Accept your spouse as he is (really!) and listen to him so that you know who the person really is. It can save you from a lot of disappointments and misunderstandings.

—*Sandra Lackey*

167

Always take time to remember why you fell in love to begin with and celebrate those reasons! It is important to take time out for "date night" once a month to reconnect. Every couple can get so caught up in "life" that they forget to take time for the things that really matter. Don't lose sight of what brought you together in the first place.

—*Sara Affonso*

168

After twenty years of being married, we are still madly in love with each other for this reason: We keep "the Light of hope" as the third party in our marriage. For us the Light is Jesus Christ. Whatever you choose as a point of light to give you hope, do it. The Light of hope will work wonders by giving you optimism during tough times. It will do three things: speak understanding and compromise when you can't find the words to clear the air; save you money spent on the marriage counselor's couch; and remind you over and over again that forgiveness and brighter days are around the corner. Don't start a home without it!

—*Sherre Bishop*

169

As you grow together you will develop "hooks" or areas of disagreement upon which you can hang other disagreements. For example, "If you would go to church more often, maybe you wouldn't be so negative." Using one hook after another causes a downward spiral making any argument 100 percent ineffective. Learn to recognize the start of a spiral and agree to stop. Go to your corners and cool off. Resolutions come from rest.

—*Steve Goetzman*

170

I do not make my wife responsible for my happiness. I own that. After being married for almost forty-four years with four daughters and nine grandchildren, we have learned that no one

can be responsible to make another person happy.
Each person is responsible for his or her own
happiness. I like Gibran's statement in the book
The Prophet: "Marriage is like an oak tree and
a cypress tree that don't stand in one another's
shadow."

—*Terry Smith*

171

"Humor, humor, humor—seeing the humor in
each other, laughing at each other's jokes (even
repeats), starting to laugh when you ought to be
mad, being able to laugh at each other's eccen-
tricities—is all part of the glue that keeps you
together.

—*Teddie Clark*

172

Always have patience with each other. Patience is the ability to endure without complaint.

—*Frances and Jack Hopper*

173

I always try to be as sharp-sighted to my husband's good points as I can be to his bad. I try to point out the good, and keep my mouth shut about the bad. I *try to,* mind you.

—*Mary Herbert Kelly*

174

Make time for each other. It's too easy to leave it to last, and then you never get to it. Staying connected makes it easier to weather the storms.

—*Jan Read*

175

Don't go to the bathroom in front of each other. *Ever!* Decorum is important.

—*Lisa and Rick Circeo*

176

Hold hands in public. Give your spouse an occasional public kiss—just a slight, tender whisp of a kiss. Nothing obvious or overt. More like a passing, private kiss that you've secretly allowed others to spy on. And don't kiss publicly too often, lest you be branded lewd, possessive, or prideful. Holding hands and an occasional openly secret kiss leaves us with the lasting certainty that we adore each other completely.

—David Lyons

177

Don't ever resort to name-calling. These are words you can truly never take back.

—Michelle West

178

We heard this at a wedding: "If you are going to argue, argue naked."

—Peg and Harry Williams

179

Forget your favorite song and find a favorite TV series that you both like. It will keep you current and connected. My husband and I have shared everything from *Lost* to *True Blood*. It's something we do once a week together and does not require leaving the house! Even better, do it in bed!

—*Susan Tyler*

180

Our wedding photographer always told us that if you and your spouse ever get into a fight and one threatens to walk out, hand that person the wedding album. This will bring to mind the happiest day of your lives and hopefully the spouse will rethink the decision. We have been married seventeen years.

—*Deborah and Stephen Hays*

181

The Lord was good to me and gave me a first-class woman. Honesty and loyalty are very important, but you need to remember to keep God in your wishes and in your dreams.

—Jack Gunter

182

You take it one day at a time and do what you can to be true to your partner. That's a full-time job.

—Bettye Gunter

183

One thing that has kept Sharon and me happy is going dancing twice a week. She goes Friday and I go on Saturday. But seriously, it is very important to find and maintain hobbies and activities you enjoy together. Working and sitting around the house aren't going to cut it for long.

—Mike Pigott

184

Ask for what you need: miracles happen.

—*Susie Ries*

185

Stephen and I have only been married a year, but one of the more helpful things we've established is not to argue while hungry. I sometimes refer to being "hangry," which is the anger that comes with hunger. So maybe, "Try to avoid having serious and important discussions if either one of you is 'hangry.'"

—*Katie Ries*

186

When you begin to have concerns of any kind, tell your spouse and talk it over. "Stuff" grows out of proportion when not talked about. This is a vital tip, in my opinion.

—*Julie Webb*

187

I will share this anonymous quotation: "Communication is to love, as blood is to the body. Without it, it dies."

—Cheryl W. Smith

188

Here are my thirteen steps to a great marriage. It originally started as ten steps but grew over the years. Obviously, it is from the man's point of view. I give it to just about every guy I know who is getting married:

1. Always be willing to compromise.
2. Quickly admit that you're wrong, even if you're not.
3. Never get in bed while you're still mad at each other.
4. Be best friends as husband and wife.
5. When you get mad or upset at each other because of potential faults, remember your own faults.

6. Don't spend large sums of money without clearing it with the other first.
7. From Ann Landers—Hold hands and hug and kiss regularly.
8. Remember: When she's wrong, she's still right.
9. Always let her drive the nicer car.
10. If you give her what she wants, then you can have anything you want, but you have to take care of her first.
11. Always call if you're gonna be late.
12. Don't give yourself a present on her birthday.
13. It's best not to hide anything. Be up front and honest—it takes the sting out of getting caught.

—Al Thomas

189

A Chinese proverb: "Do not use a hatchet to remove a fly from your spouse's forehead."

—Jean Hastings

190

Remember, it is not a 50-50 deal. It takes 125 percent from both persons ever to get to the kind of understanding that will be required to keep going. You have to give a lot more than you think you should.

—*Greer Broemel*

191

I ask myself, "How important is this?" when I find myself digging in over an issue. I realize that I don't have to have an opinion about *everything* that goes on. Let things go and pick your battles, is my advice.

—*Maureen Turnbull*

192

Don't forget that laughter and humor go a long way.

—*Robbie McDermott*

193

Two people in a marriage create a third party, a relationship. Nurture and love the relationship. It is the most important thing in your life. Also, allow yourself to be loved.

—Tom Turnbull

194

Find somebody compatible, and be willing to compromise. Have a sense of humor, but take the relationship seriously.

—Wayne Wood

195

Married forty years: "Trust and laughter. Without the trust you won't get far to begin with. The laughter has been our friend through illness, raising kids, personal issues, and the trials and tribulations that we all go through.

—Errol and Helen Dunn

196

Guys, no matter how good her intentions and promises that she would never do this, at some point your wife will turn into her mother. Ladies, ditto. Your husband will become his father. Get ready.

—*Ken Goodrich*

197

Actually, praise and appreciation. I think all men need that. Maybe all people. I tell him specifically *how* he is terrific. Telling him he is a gentle grandfather means more than saying he is a wonderful grandfather. He hears it better.

—*Maureen Turnbull*

198

From the book *Advice to a Young Wife from an Old Mistress,* which I have found to be most insightful: "All newcomers to marriage are inescapably beginners, cheerfully certain that they have arrived at a triumphant culmination instead of a precarious takeoff. Swearing to love forever is like promising to feel perpetually any other emotion, fear or sorrow, admiration or joy. What one can swear is to go on being worth loving, a vow that is more flexible, more attainable, and more true."

—*Janet Davies*

199

Also from *Advice to a Young Wife from an Old Mistress:* "Wives should have money of their own. Only slaves and very young children are without a source of income. Dependency, no matter how construed, is simply not grown up. A sharp imbalance of money hinders free relationship, forcing it to make do on what the poorer partner can afford, else turning that one into a sycophant. Having your own money is not only freedom, it is freedom from judgment and control from the one who holds it, in short for attaining a fuller stature."

—*Janet Davies*

200

Here is a short, but profound, bit of wisdom (from Ruth Bell Graham): "A happy marriage is the union of two good forgivers."

—Allison Beasley

201

Advice from 1886, attributed to Jane Wells: Let your love be stronger than your hate and anger. Learn the wisdom of compromise, for it is better to bend a little than to break. Believe the best rather than the worst. People have a way of living up or down to your opinion of them. Remember that true friendship is the basis for any lasting relationship. The person you choose to marry is deserving of the courtesies and kindnesses you bestow on your friends.

—Jennifer Rawlings

202

My favorite marriage advice, from Cokie and

Tom Roberts: "Never to forget those three crucial little words: 'Maybe I'm wrong.'"

—*Laura Cooper*

203

Treat your husband like a king. Just make sure he knows you are the queen.

—*Janet Hogan*

204

Before deciding to marry, take a good look at your proposed partner and decide if you want to have breakfast with that person every day for the rest of your life.

—*Tom Turnbull*

205

We recommend the excellent book *The Most Important Year of a Woman's Life/The Most Important Year of a Man's Life,* by Susan and Mark DeVries and Bobbie and Robert Wolgemuth. Jeff

and I both read it in the months of our engage-
ment, though it is equally fitting to read during
the first year of marriage (or as a refresher course
down the road!). One of the chapters in the book
is about "normals" and how we all have our own,
unique, often quirky "normals" that we tend to
hold very close to our hearts and cling to tightly. I
nodded in agreement as I was reading, but it was
not until we returned from the honeymoon that
the profound truth of that insight really struck
me. The first day in our new home we were closing ourselves in for the night and Jeff turned the
blinds *up* I always turned them *down* and could
not believe that anyone would think it was a good
idea to do the opposite! We had a good laugh
about it, and have had several similar conversa-
tions in the past six months. Clashing "normals"
were hitting us left and right after our November
wedding as we spent holidays with each other's
families for the first time. Turns out we string
the lights on the Christmas tree from opposite
ends! It was a huge blessing to have read this
valuable insight into how to handle these situations—laughter and respect are usually equally
important—and to know that not seeing eye to

eye about how to trim the Christmas tree or how to fold towels does not mean we are hopelessly incompatible, but rather quite simply that we are just two individuals with different lives up to this point who decided it would be more enjoyable to do life hand in hand, as long as we both shall live!

—*Caroline Rossini*

206

They say two can live as cheaply as one and staying married is cheaper than getting divorced, if you can manage it. We were married in the Episcopal Church twenty-five years ago and pre-marital counseling was required. Our priest took that very seriously, and we had to do a segment on fighting fair. I thought this was pretty stupid since I knew, of course, that *we* would never fight. The most useful tidbit we picked up was that you were never allowed to use "biological warfare" in an argument. That meant you could not bring in any family members. So phrases such as, "you're just like your father"; "you're turning into your mother"; "That's exactly what your brother would do," would be totally out. That turned out to be very useful advice.

—*Jennifer Johnston*

207

Our minister, Carson Fraser, told us in our pre-marital counseling that "Jesus should be the number-one person" in our marriage. Now, I know that without praying for forgiveness and guidance I never would have made it this far.

—*Greer Broemel*

208

"Aunt Marian and Uncle Craig's Recipe for a Happy Married Life":

- Don't argue about the small stuff—and almost everything is small.
- When he cooks, make sure you compliment it!
- Work hard to enjoy your in-laws.

- Say "Yes, Dear" at least 6 times a day.
- Say "I love You" at least 8 times a day.
- When in doubt, take a deep breath.
- Keep up the small kindnesses to each other—just like when you first met.
- Avoid criticizing how your mate does a task unless you are willing to do it.
- Work to improve those habits of yours that you know annoy your mate.
- Work to accept the annoying habits of your mate.
- Remember that a 50/50 partnership refers to your whole life together, not to each day or week.

—Marian Ott

209

Fights indicate you are intimate enough to have disagreements. When we celebrated our twenty-fifth year of marriage, our son Ted said, "Congratulations on 23 years of happy marriage!" We do have fights, some pretty terrible, but we always resolve them (or agree to live with the differences) before going to bed.

—*Teddie Clark*

210

Gregg and I have been married for twelve years. We are college sweethearts who have successfully endured medical school, the birth of two wonderful daughters, and all that hell and high waters bring in Nashville. We both agree that to ensure marital happiness, one should not call the mother-in-law a "witch," or anything that may rhyme with witch.

—*Amy Jo Shepard*

211

Only certain things are worth arguing about. Think about whether the issue is something you would even remember five years from now. If not, just let it go.

—*Larry McCormack*

212

I have been married twice (once for forty-six years, and now for five years). I like to think this gives me a total of fifty-one years of marital experience. One of the most important things I have learned over this long period of time is that it's more important to graciously leave the battlefield over who is right about something before it gets really ugly. Because it really isn't a win if the vanquished feels it was a mistake to marry the other person. Finally, if you gain enough self-confidence, you'll be content in the satisfaction that you actually were right!

—Marlin Sanders

213

Thought for the Day: A married man should forget his mistakes. There's no use in two people remembering the same thing!

—From the Internet, "Why Men Are Happier
Than Women"

214

Don't be resentful for lack of help if you've never taken the time to ask for help.

—*Liza Graves*

215

My husband is my best friend, but we also have outside interests. This is very important in a marriage. I need my girl time and he needs his guy time. Married thirty years and looking forward to thirty more.

—*Tracy McClimans*

216

Laugh together every day. Laughter makes you feel better and can cover a multitude of sins!

—*Misty Green*

217

If you are in a blended marriage, do not try to

be a mother to your spouse's child or children. Be their friend and it will be on their terms. You will be very unhappy if you have expectations of having a mother-child relationship with them. They will decide what they want from you, and you need to be that friend or support system for them because you love your spouse. Remember, there are very few functional families, if any, particularly in a divorced situation!

—Ann

218

Put God first and pray together and for each other. Make each other a priority and always try to make sure the needs of your spouse are met. You have to communicate to make this happen, and if you need something, you have to say so. Be best friends and genuinely enjoy each other's company and companionship. I've been married for five years and I love my husband so much more than the day I married him!

—Liz

219

When it comes to blended families, particularly to women who marry men with children (but who have no children themselves): In my experience, keeping my mouth shut when I disagreed with the way my husband and his ex-wife were raising their child was the best thing I could do. I had to learn this over time and by making mistakes, of course, but I do believe the less I interfered, the better. It was best for me to tend to my own business and stay out of theirs, even when I wanted to give them all kinds of "advice" on how to do it perfectly!

—Amy Dennison

220

If you want him to do things with which you have more familiarity, especially if it's something you'll want him to do often in the future (like taking care of a new baby), don't criticize or "correct" him if his way of doing things happens to be different from yours (but is otherwise safe). Your way is not necessarily the only way, even though you may think so. Even if you've learned through trial and error that there is a better way, fight the urge to say "You're doing it wrong." The response is often, "Fine, *you* do it." Unless safety is an issue, if you can't stand to watch him do it differently without criticizing, quietly leave the room. And two, choose the right person to begin with.

—*Beth Scott*

221

Humor, hard work, and luck.

—*Shannon Barton*

222

Laugh often—at shared experiences, at jokes, at crazy things you see or hear, at each other, and most important, at yourself.

—*Laura Riley*

223

Married sixty years: Unselfishness on the part of both. Remember to keep your marriage vows—"in sickness and in health"—"for richer or poorer." Cherish each other's friends as well as joint friends. Also share similar backgrounds; have compatible interests; observe mutual respect; avoid jealousy. Belonging to and attending church is a big plus.

—*Mr. and Mrs. John W. Barton*

224

Married sixty-one years: I learned to say I was sorry even if I knew I hadn't done anything wrong.

—*Corinne Wilson*

225

Offer consistently positive statements to and about your spouse. Avoid focusing on a shortcoming of your spouse, but rather see any challenge as a collective challenge that will be addressed and solved by both of you.

—*Keith Wood*

226

Throw the word *fair* out the window. In one year of a marriage, one person may need 99 percent of the love, effort, or focus of the other; another year, it may be just the opposite.

—*Rinnie Wood*

227

Get married, get in a Ryder truck and move 2,000 miles from your families, and start your life together. That way you have to depend on each other from the beginning. You just have each other and you can't run home to Mama.

—*Susan Leathers*

228

We were driving along and listening to the radio and there was a psychiatrist and a psychologist and a priest discussing divorce and what caused it—money, family pressure, in-laws, sex—all of that. And the psychiatrist said, "No, that is not it. It is boredom." That said so much. I would never have divorced, because I never knew what John was going to do next. We always kept things going. The whole idea is to keep your life interesting—which we did.

—*Nancy Katz*

229

In our wedding instruction in 1952, Peyton Williams told us to be aware of the three kinds of love: *Filia,* brother love, friendship; *eros,* romantic love; and *agape,* sacrificial or unconditional love. At various times one may be stronger or weaker. My dad's way of saying this was that "50/50 won't cut it. It must be 100/100."

—*Shirley Lechleiter*

230

Keep your mind open to the possibility that the person you marry is not exactly who you think he or she is. Dating, no matter how long a courtship, is a time for you to show your best side. Don't be discouraged or frightened by the bits and pieces of the other person's personality that will emerge that are less than date-face perfect. Don't be intimidated by character traits that emerge that you, and possibly your spouse, never knew existed. Remember that if you are to stay in a committed relationship with someone for decades, peeling back the layers will keep it interesting. Wouldn't it be boring if you and your spouse stayed exactly the same year after year? Hang on tightly during these discovery times to the core values that attracted you to your spouse in the first place and learn to welcome each stage of personal growth. The upside to being open to discovery is that your spouse will surprise you with new skills depending on your stage of the game. Who knew my hardworking, serious husband would be the one to crack my teenagers up and lighten the mood when our family needed it? Allowing yourself and your spouse to change keeps things fresh and interesting, and frankly, is inevitable.

—*Cathi Aycock*

231

The one bit of advice I remember getting before we married thirty-four years ago was—if you ask your husband to do some chore around the house—and the way he does it doesn't meet your standards—don't go behind him and "fix" it, or he will never want to do it again.

—*Evon Lee*

232

We center our marriage on one word—*edify.* This is especially important in speech. We don't say or do anything that will not edify the other. That goes for public and private. Even when George and I have a disagreement, we always place the other one at the center of respect. Our goal is to build each other up at all times. One day, I heard a friend ask George if I ever nagged him. He gave the sweetest response: "No . . . even when it might be something I could twist into nagging, I know she loves me and is only trying to help me be the best person I can be." My heart just melted and I think of that often. Words are powerful, and loving words are the Superman of language!

—*Tammy Algood*

233

Cooking and cleaning up are a gift of unparalleled value (for both parties). The only thing better is going to the grocery, *and* cooking and cleaning up!

—*Rinnie Wood*

234

Ladies: he is not, and never shall be, a mind reader. If you do not tell him what you are thinking, he will never, ever come up with it all by himself. "You should have known" is the most inane thought a woman can have in her head about any man.

—*Ken Goodrich*

235

Always treat each other with respect; communicate honestly and openly; don't be afraid to seek professional help if you reach an impasse; try to never do anything that causes mistrust. And learn to say "yes, m'am"—a lot.

—*Jim Tyree*

236

Pay attention to how you sound on the telephone when your spouse calls—not only for your spouse's benefit but also for those (such as your children or friends) who are in listening distance. It's so much better to sound thrilled to hear from them, than annoyed or too busy to take the call.

—*Marsha Luey*

237

In our seventy years of marriage, we have had the opportunity to observe a large number of marriages, both good and bad. We have come to the conclusion that there are several main factors that determine a good marriage:

- Religion or the lack thereof: It is evident that those who have the same religious beliefs are more compatible than those with difference of opinions.
- Money: both the lack of and too much of. The lack of money brings on hardships that some couples don't seem to be able to cope with. The excess of money encourages excessive spending—and the problem of focusing on the money instead of each other.
- Sex: Here again we have a problem of the lack of. I just read recently a survey that said 64 percent of wives would rather read or do housework than have sex with their husbands. I'm not sure how accurate this is, but if it is, then this could explain the amount of infidelity with some couples.

- Communication: This one is as important as any of the others. When there is a break-down of communication, the relationship suffers.
- Kindness and consideration.
- Of course, the greatest of all is true love for each other.

—John and Alice Hall

238

A friend (now divorced) always said no gift to a lady includes a cord. If it included a cord (a sweeper, mixer, hedge clipper) it was not only *not* a gift but an insult to any self-respecting woman.

—Terry Clements

239

Respect each other's body clocks. My natural sleep patterns, which were to stay up late and sleep late, drove Jim crazy at first, but then we agreed I wouldn't get mad at him if he couldn't stay up past nine and he wouldn't get mad at me if I wanted to sleep until eleven in the morning. Now, when we travel, I return to my go-to-bed-earlier, get-up-earlier routine. Thank goodness most of the rest of the world doesn't open up their museums or stores until ten! Jim still gets up early, but after a couple of trips abroad, I realized I would have to give him a job or he would drive me crazy between seven and nine in the morning. We now have approximately twenty-five won-derful journals written by Jim from all over the world. He gets up early, has a cup of coffee, and writes in his journal until I get up! One of these days I'm going to compile them all and give "Journeys with Jim" to family and friends.

—*Lissa Kelly*

240

From day one of our marriage, I told Jim I would never spend time worrying about trusting him. My motto was I will trust you until you give me a reason not to. But if you ever betray that trust, that will be the end of our relationship. No second chances. So far, so good!

—*Lissa Kelly*

241

You have to have a lot in common to begin with. That notion of "opposites attract" doesn't really hold true. There have to be some very strong agreements on basic things. For instance, politics, leisure time activities, hobbies. And your educational background, intellect, and sense of humor have to be pretty much in sync.

—*Lissa Kelly*

242

I don't believe in the statement that people don't change. People can always change bad habits if they are constantly being reinforced to behave better. For example, early in our marriage Jim had a habit of just leaving his clothes on the floor, even when the laundry hamper was sitting right there! I know this seems trivial, but it caused a lot of angst on my part, because I just felt like I wasn't being respected. So, at first I asked him to please put his clothes in the laundry hamper. He continued to drop them on the floor. After a few more weeks, I told him that if he continued dropping his clothes on the floor, I would throw them away. He didn't learn. I started throwing away his underwear, one or two a week. After a while he asked me what had happened to his underwear. I told him if it was on the floor I had thrown it away. Problem solved.

—*Lissa Kelly*

243

Always establish early on that keeping your marriage together is the most important thing for your family. We started having a date night when Kathleen was one month old. Every week we got a babysitter. We may not have always wanted to go out, but we did and were sometimes home by eight. Jim also established a routine with Kathleen when she was about three months old. He would take her somewhere every Saturday morning and that would be my morning to sleep in. They would go to Pancake Pantry, the airport to watch planes take off, McDonald's, the zoo, the library, anywhere. They had their special time together, and I think that made such a huge difference in their relationship and I had some alone time.

—*Lissa Kelly*

244

Avoid saying the following:

- Pull my finger.
- I wouldn't say your butt looks fat in those jeans, just bigger.
- That chili (insert any food here) was good . . . not as good as my mom's though.
- Do you know how to get the skidmarks out of my boxers?
- Honey, I'm sorry your aunt died, but what

can I possibly do about it from the golf course?

—*Rick Circeo*

245

What my father always told me when I was planning my wedding: "You have to want to have a marriage, not just a wedding. Remember the difference."

—*Lisa Circeo*

246

I'm a firm believer in the idea that the way the couple goes about planning the wedding—and whether they agree on the planning—is a very important guide to how the marriage is going to go.

—*Wayne Wood*

247

I don't bring up past grievances when having an argument.

—*Maureen Turnbull*

248

The guy you're marrying is the guy you're marrying. You are sadly delusional if you think you can actually change him once you've got him married to you. If you love him as he is, rather than any utopian fantasy you have of his becoming, you will still love him thirty years from now.

—*Ken Goodrich*

249

From *The Prophet,* by Kahlil Gibran, in the chapter titled "On Marriage": "Let there be spaces in your togetherness, and let the winds of the heavens dance between you." Rod and I have so many similarities and so many significant differences. It's easy to rejoice in the similarities. Learning to appreciate and really embrace the differences is my goal and my growth edge. This struggle seems to be a drag, but it's really the path to becoming the whole person, and wife, that I long to be.

—Jane Hardy

250

A quotation I love but can't remember exactly goes something like this: "A good marriage is not about being lucky or passionate—it's about being grateful and forgiving."

—Jo Dee Prichard

251

I would say that mutual love and caring is #1, and a date night is most important.

—Martha Brandon

252

My daddy has always said that what has worked for him and my mother all these years is that Mom waits on him hand and foot and he gives her everything he has.

—*Julie Barnes*

253

Spoil your spouse every day.

—*Ottie Paslay*

254

Try always to be understanding. Oh, and remember to say "I love you" every day!

—*Barbara Paslay*

255

My best advice may be that, when you come home from work, don't just come home physically. Bring your mind home as well and do something special every once in a while for no reason at all.

—*Mike Paslay*

256

Learn fast that the grass is not greener on the other side of the fence!

—*Lulu Elam*

257

Conchie and I were married about 200 yards from the house that I grew up in. The wedding was simple and the reception was just held in the churchyard. At the end of the festivities, Conchie changed her clothes and tossed her wedding dress over her arm for the walk back to my old house. Just before we reached the door, we were stopped by an elderly woman who noticed (Conchie) wearing jeans and hauling a long white dress over her shoulder. Although I had lived on that quiet street for over twenty years I had never before seen this woman. After inquiring about our wedding she gave us some parting advice. She said that before her husband passed away they had been happily married for over fifty years. Speaking in a tone that made it clear she knew from experience, she simply said, "It's not all give, it's not all take. It's give and take." Every time we reach a point in our marriage that we need a gentle reminder, we echo that refrain from a moment in our marriage that was less than an hour old.

—*John Shackleford*

258

After several years of marriage, there is no way I'm training another husband, so I will just keep the one I have!

—*Joyce Brown*

259

Our advice: separate checking accounts. Not only do couples avoid issues involving different styles of record-keeping, but each person maintains some financial independence.

—*Marcia Clarkson*

260

Be united on issues with children so that they get a consistent message and know you are a team. Another is to do something with your spouse that he or she loves but you are not interested in at all, and do it without complaining or making it sound like a burden. You may find you really are a Titans fan or great ballroom dancer.

—*Julia Morris*

261

If you find that you show more courtesy to friends and strangers than to your own spouse, reassess your priorities.

—*Janet Hogan*

262

After having a fight with your spouse, it's always good to gargle with Jack Daniel's—then swallow as much as you can of it.

—*Robbie McDermott*

263

We have a picture hanging in the hallway of Tom when he was a little boy. If I glance at that when I'm mad at him it reminds me that he isn't always a jerk.

—*Maureen Turnbull*

Celebrity Section

My good friend Beverly Keel married for the first time at age forty-one and was the celebrity columnist for the *Tennessean* at the time of her wedding. Here is advice some of

Nashville's most famous names shared with her for her column on how to have a happy marriage.

264

You have to have open, honest, and consistent communication.

—*Reba McEntire*

265

Take your wife coffee every morning. Everyone's day starts off better that way.

—*Nashville mayor Karl Dean*

266

Five tips:

1. Separate bathrooms. If you can't afford a second one, register (for wedding gifts) at Home Depot and build it! It's that important.
2. If one snores, get a snore guard.

3. Read *Men Are from Mars, Women Are from Venus.*
4. In an argument, never take away the other person's dignity. (Dr. Phil personally told me this.)
5. Marriage counseling.

—*Naomi Judd*

267

Spend quality quiet time together. After an argument, take time to cool down before you kiss and make up. Put God before your spouse.

—*Josh Turner*

268

Never stop flirting with your spouse. You will go through highs and lows, tough times and great times. Through them all, all your spouse needs to know is that you are into them as much today as you were during that first date.

—*News anchor Bob Mueller*

269

I feel like a happy marriage probably just takes a lot of love and a lot of luck.

—*Community leader Clare Armistead*

270

A happy marriage is embracing each moment as if it were your last together, and communication. There's nothing complex about it. There's no 10 rules or 10 ways of keeping a happy marriage. It's keeping an open line of communication and keeping real with that. You say you communicate, but you really don't. There are things my wife will say to me that I've thought, *Why didn't you talk to me about it?* She thought I wouldn't understand.

—*NFL great Eddie George*

271

You'd better be friends and they'd better make you laugh because it's like having the world's longest roommate. It's like you get a roommate and they don't move out after four years. My wife Allyson and I just laugh all the time. She is the funniest person I know; I am just happy to listen to her talk.

—Longtime WSIX radio man Gerry House

272

Make Jesus Christ a part of your union. If I had prayed to him throughout my marriage (to Alan) to protect us from anything that would draw us away from each other, I don't believe we would have gone through the heartaches that we did. (But then, I wouldn't have the story to tell that I do.) So you see, He always has a plan and a purpose for everything, if you belong to Him. The closer we are to Him, the more we exhibit the fruits of his Spirit to others (our spouses), which are love, joy, peace, patience, kindness, goodness, and self-control.

—Denise Jackson, author

273

I never set out to change the person I married, nor did he set out to change me. That would have been a real stumbling block. I think divine intervention came to me because I chose a man who had no agenda, only to take care of me and protect me and help me be who I am. We try to never go to bed mad at each other, no matter what has happened during the day.

—Brenda Lee

274

I always say liking each other helps and respecting each other is imperative, but it goes beyond that. Communication, honesty, and loyalty are key. The ability to put someone else's needs or feelings first sometimes. Being able to compromise. Having the same values. Knowing that you are going to have bad days and a rough patch here and there, but it doesn't mean it's over; it's just a rough patch. Feeling like the relationship is a safe place for you to be your true self. Being able to want the best for someone and trying to build them up, not tear them down. Being able to overlook the little things. Being able to appreciate the little things. And most important, a sense of humor. I guess I just described someone that you could call your true friend.

—Martina McBride

More Big-Name Advice

Following are nuggets of advice offered by an assortment of well-known persons, from Ambrose Bierce to Zig Ziglar.

275

I've been thinking about one of the secrets to a happy marriage, and this is something I believe: When it comes to coping with hard times and adversity, there are three kinds of people in the world: People who, in the face of difficulty, can still find something to laugh about. People who, given some time and perspective, can laugh about it. And people who will never be able to laugh about it. Well, life is a whole lot sweeter if you marry one of the folks in the first two groups! It doesn't matter when you laugh, just as long as you do.

—*Singer-songwriter Mark Selby ("There's Your Trouble" and "Blue on Black")*

276

The "secret" is to always feel like you married "up." My husband, Mark, is always telling people he married "up" when we tied the knot, but the truth is, I feel like I'm the lucky one and totally out of my league ever since he chose me.

—*Singer-songwriter Tia Sillers ("I Hope You Dance")*

277

You really gotta love each other. Living with each other is no day at the beach every day. My mother said that most people live parallel lives but that Chris and I are dovetails. I thought that was wonderful. Another thing—being right all the time is a recipe for disaster. The world is full of lonely people who are right all the time.

—*Singer-songwriter-author Marshall*
Chapman

278

Marriage, n. A community consisting of a master, a mistress, and two slaves, making in all, two.

—*Ambrose Bierce,* The Devil's Dictionary,
1911

279

Success in marriage does not come merely through finding the right mate, but through being the right mate.

—*Barnett R. Brickner, rabbi*

280

The bonds of matrimony are like any other bonds—they mature slowly.

—*Peter De Vries, novelist*

281

Husbands are like fires. They go out when unattended.

—Zsa Zsa Gabor

282

One advantage of marriage is that, when you fall out of love with him or he falls out of love with you, it keeps you together until you fall in again.

—Judith Viorst, writer

283

Sometimes I wonder if men and women really suit each other. Perhaps they should live next door and just visit now and then.

—Katharine Hepburn

284

If you made a list of the reasons why any couple got married, and another list of the reasons for their divorce, you'd have a hell of a lot of overlapping.

—*Mignon McLaughlin,* The Neurotic's Notebook, *1960*

285

There is no substitute for the comfort supplied by the utterly taken-for-granted relationship.

—*Iris Murdoch, writer*

286

Love seems the swiftest, but it is the slowest of all growths. No man or woman really knows what perfect love is until they have been married a quarter of a century.

—*Mark Twain*

287

Never feel remorse for what you have thought about your wife; she has thought much worse things about you.

—*Jean Rostand, biologist,* Le Mariage, *1927*

288

Marriage is a great institution, but I'm not ready for an institution.

—*Mae West*

289

Don't marry the person you think you can live with; marry only the individual you think you can't live without.

—*James C. Dobson*

290

Never marry for money. Ye'll borrow it cheaper.

—*Scottish Proverb*

291

What counts in making a happy marriage is not so much how compatible you are, but how you deal with incompatibility.

—*Leo Tolstoy*

292

My mother once told me that if a married couple puts a penny in a pot for every time they make love in the first year, and takes a penny out every time after that, they'll never get all the pennies out of the pot.

—*Armistead Maupin,* Tales of the City, *1978*

293

What greater thing is there for two human souls than to feel that they are joined together to strengthen each other in all labour, to minister to each other in all sorrow, to share with each other in all gladness, to be one with each other in the silent unspoken memories?

—*George Eliot*

294

The more you invest in a marriage, the more valuable it becomes.

—*Amy Grant*

295

There is nothing more admirable than two people who see eye-to-eye keeping house as man and wife, confounding their enemies, and delighting their friends.

—*Homer, ninth century* B.C.

296

I have no way of knowing whether or not you married the wrong person, but I do know that many people have a lot of wrong ideas about marriage and what it takes to make that marriage happy and successful. I'll be the first to admit that it's possible that you did marry the wrong person. However, if you treat the wrong person like the right person, you could well end up having married the right person after all. On the other hand, if you marry the right person, and treat that person wrong, you certainly will have ended up marrying the wrong person. I also know that it is far more important to be the right kind of person than it is to marry the right person. In short, whether you married the right or wrong person is primarily up to you.

—*Zig Ziglar*

297

I am convinced that if we as a society work diligently in every other area of life and neglect the family, it would be analogous to straightening deck chairs on the *Titanic*.

—*Stephen Covey*

298

Love is what you've been through with somebody.

—*James Thurber*

299

Our greatest weakness lies in giving up. The most certain way to succeed is always to try just one more time.

—*Thomas Edison*

300

There is no greater happiness for a man than approaching a door at the end of a day knowing someone on the other side of that door is waiting for the sound of his footsteps.

—*Ronald Reagan*

301

Chains do not hold a marriage together. It is threads, hundreds of tiny threads which sew people together through the years. That is what makes a marriage last—more than passion or even sex!

—*Simone Signoret*

302

Perhaps the most unfortunate and damaging phrase for women's well-being ever to catch hold is Steinem's "A woman needs a man like a fish needs a bicycle." Who can blame men riding off on their bikes—waving and smiling as they head off for a bit more fishing. We need desperately to correct that. We need to say, "I want you and I need you—right here by my side raising these kids. Get off the damn bicycle and stay right here."

—*Diane Sollee, smartmarriages.com*

303

Try praising your wife, even if it does frighten her at first.

—Billy Sunday

304

One last point about how talking to your man is different from talking to your girlfriend. By and large, a man wants the bottom line. Cut the amount of prelude by approximately ninety percent, and you'll get it just about right. Instead of saying, "Honey, my mom went in and the doctor diagnosed varicose veins. She's going to have to get them stripped, which will make it very difficult for her to walk for a couple of weeks. As you know, she lives all alone now, and the only person who can help her is Mrs. Jenkins, who just visits twice a week, on Thursdays and Fridays. Mom's going to need more help than that." Trust me, you've probably lost him by that point. Instead, try this: "Honey, my mom is having surgery next week and needs some time to recover. Do you mind if she stays with us for a few days?" If he wants more information, he'll ask for it. Keep it short.

—*Kevin Leman,* Making Sense of the Men in Your Life

305

Don't just follow your heart, because your heart can be deceived . . . *lead* your heart.

—Fireproof, *the movie*

306

By all means, marry. If you get a good wife, you'll become happy; if you get a bad one, you'll become a philosopher.

—*Socrates*

307

I was married by a judge. I should have asked for a jury.

—*Groucho Marx*

308

You can't take care of others until you take care of yourself. You need balance and joy in your life.

—*Dr. Phil in* O magazine, *June 2010*

309

Macel and I decided years ago, we are going to do whatever we have to to make this marriage work. Learn to talk without fighting. You can win the argument and lose your marriage! Marriage is a relationship, not a contest. There are no winners, unless you both win! Talk together, pray together, then play together.

—Jerry Falwell, Sermon, TRBC.org,
"Maximizing Your Marriage," Macel and Jerry
Falwell Marriage Profile

310

Ruth and I don't have a perfect marriage, but we have a great one. . . . For a married couple to expect perfection in each other is unrealistic.

—Billy Graham, BillyGraham.com, Ruth and
Billy Graham Marriage Profile

311

Let him know you're happy: I smile whenever I see him. He always knows how thrilled I am that he's there with me.

—Melanie Griffith, married to Antonio
Banderas, Redbook.com

312

I knew couples who'd been married almost forever—forty, fifty, sixty years. Seventy-two, in one case. They'd be tending each other's illnesses, filling in each other's faulty memories, dealing with the money troubles or the daughter's suicide, or the grandson's drug addiction. And I was beginning to suspect that it made no difference whether they'd married the right person. Finally, you're just with who you're with. You've signed on with her, put in a half century with her, grown to know her as well as you know yourself or even better, and she's become the right person. Or the only person, might be more to the point. I wish someone had told me that earlier. I'd have hung on then; I swear I would.

—*Anne Tyler,* A Patchwork Planet

313

In all of our fifty years together, Eydie and I have never . . . [long, long pause] . . . had a meaningful conversation!

—*Steve Lawrence, when asked by Johnny Carson about the secret to his fifty-year marriage to Eydie Gorme*

314

I learned fairly early in my marriage that I did not have to confide everything on my mind to my husband; this would be putting on him burdens which I was supposed to carry myself. When a bride insists on telling her lover everything, I suspect she is looking for a father, not a husband.

Some of my life was mine to be known by me alone.

> —*Madeleine L'Engle,* Two-Part Invention:
> The Story of a Marriage, *Hugh Franklin and
> Madeleine L'Engle Marriage Profile*

315

A love which depends solely on romance, on the combustion of two attracting chemistries, tends to fizzle out . . . A long-term marriage has to move beyond chemistry to compatibility, to friendship, to companionship. It is certainly not that passion disappears, but that it is conjoined with other ways of love.

> —*Madeleine L'Engle,* Two-Part Invention:
> The Story of a Marriage, *Hugh Franklin and
> Madeleine L'Engle Marriage Profile*

316

You have to keep creating a marriage. We talk about everything. We grow and change together, because nothing ever stays the same; you've got to continue evolving.

—*Kelly Preston, married to John Travolta,*
Redbook.com

317

According to a University of North Carolina study, the more often you feel gratitude toward your significant other, the stronger your relationship will be.

318

To keep your marriage brimming
With love in the wedding cup,
Whenever you're wrong, admit it;
Whenever you're right, shut up.

—*Ogden Nash*

Married Fifty Years or More

Whenever you seek advice, I think it's always wise to ask the experts in the field you are interested in. So one year, for a Valentine's Day piece for my newspaper, I interviewed couples who had been married fifty years or more. I asked them to share any secrets of how their marriages had lasted so long, and for tidbits of advice for younger people considering marriage or just starting out in meaningful relationships. Here's what they had to say:

319

"It is a lot of give and take. Most of the time the woman is giving and the man is taking. We take it one day at a time. I was fifteen and he was seventeen when we married. We were always taught till death do you part. Divorce was never discussed in our house. When he was young he was high-tempered, and I didn't say anything—if you don't say anything, you don't have to take anything back. He comes first, he is spoiled, but he rubs my back every night."

—*Opal and Gene Harper, married sixty-two years*

320

"We married in 1937—I was sixteen when we married, and he kinda brought me up like he wanted to," said Margie, eighty-five.

The reason for all of the divorces these days, Cecil, ninety-two, says, is simply "selfishness" and the fact that "a lot of people don't go to church and do the right thing. You need to live right and like you are supposed to—you have an oath and you are obligated to remember that. You need to treat each other like you want to be treated," he said.

"The Lord has been good to us. We never go to bed angry," said Margie.

—*Cecil and Margie Carter*

321

"Treat each other with kindness, love, and respect. Just work it out together. Don't fuss, talk things over," said Ollie.

"We stay mad an hour or two and then that's it, and it's fun to make up," Jack added.

—Jack and Ollie Watson, married
sixty-four years

322

Roy laughed as he summed up his secret to a long, happy marriage: "Keep your mouth shut! There's no point in arguing because she's gonna be right anyway."

And if and when you have a little spat, Rose says it might be a good idea to "stay apart a little while. He's been known to walk around or drive around (to cool off) and then we drop it."

—Rose and Roy Brummitt, married
fifty-two years

323

The Paschalls say that couples planning to get married should "seek some spiritual guidance" before they take the plunge. And the best way to resolve conflict in the relationship, Julius says, is to "walk out and get by yourself for a while."

"Look at it in different ways and concentrate on the good" in the relationship, Doris added. "I always say, 'this too shall pass' and it usually does."

Julius chimed in with another successful strategy when times are tough: "A lot of counting to ten . . . twenty if necessary."

—Julius and Doris Paschall, married
fifty-two years

324

"Be considerate of each other and think of each other first," said Mae.

"It's a matter of love," said Clyde. "And you have to be willing to forgive."

—Clyde and Mae Dean, married
fifty-eight years

325

"We love each other and have been able to work out our differences through the years," Billie says, "and we are Christians and I think that helps. I'll give in one time and the next time he will. If I want anything fairly expensive, I will talk it over with him and he will do the same with me."

—Robert and Billie Ensley, married sixty-five years

326

"I give and he takes," Dorothy said.

Glen chimed in with "you've heard that Johnny Cash line from *Hee Haw*—'We've never had a fuss in our home. . . . We go outside.'"

—Dorothy and Glen Dorris, of Hendersonville, married fifty-eight years

327

"I'm the boss," says Perry. "I make sure that everything she wants gets done." Ellen says the secret is "You need to keep your husband busy. And when you go to bed at night, always kiss goodnight. We always kiss goodbye when we leave each other."

—*Perry and Ellen Harper, married fifty years*

328

"We are just made for each other," Lorraine says, and advises young people to "be really careful who you marry. It is for good."

—*Ernest and Lorraine Thompson, married*
fifty-three years

329

"I think it was different when we were young—we knew it was for life," said Hazel, who described her husband as "the easiest-to-get-along-with person that God ever made."

Whitey's advice to new or soon-to-be husbands: "You've got to learn to say, 'yes, ma'am', 'no ma'am,' 'thank you ma'am,' 'please,' and 'I'll do it right now' and you won't have any problems."

—Hazel and Whitey Ireland, married
fifty-nine years

330

"There is a lot of give and take," said Virginia. "It is a two-way street. You have got to go along with each other's ideas and hit a happy medium."

"When we said 'I do' we didn't say it was just for tomorrow," Joe said. "You gotta tie the knot where it can't be untied."

—Joe (Moon) and Virginia Smith, married
sixty years

Family Advice

Here is what my husband, our daughters, their husbands, their new in-laws, my brother, my aunt, and my cousin came up with after I insisted that our family and extended family members share their advice. I hope you will indulge me.

331

My husband Bill Hance:

1. Marry someone like my Mary . . . (I did not make him say this.)
2. Share the cooking.
3. Make the bed every morning.
4. Don't burn the toast.
5. Be first to say you're sorry . . . if you can't be the first, be the second.
6. Look both ways before going through a green light or intersection . . . always.

332

Our daughter Elizabeth and her husband, Chad:

1. Cook together, and for each other.
2. Get a dog before you have children, maybe two dogs.

3. Keep each other laughing and don't take everything so seriously!
4. Keep separate bank accounts, but save money together!
5. Enjoy time together but find time for yourself, such as boys night and girls night!

333

Our daughter, Anna Hance Tefel:

1. Do not expect the situation to always be fair; much of the time it will not be fair, but it's about giving, taking, and understanding.
2. Compliment each other often, especially in public (the best piece of advice I got when I got married—from Beth Stein—I'm still working on this one).
3. Always remember . . . you are a team!
4. Exercise often.
5. Pay attention to comings and goings—always greet and part with a X&O.

334

Anna's husband Santi Tefel:

If you are going to marry a "daddy's girl," make sure you are friends with Daddy!

335

Anna's in-laws and Santi's parents, Rey and Pilar Tefel:

1. Never do anything that you cannot tell your partner about.
2. With God in the center, you can do anything together because it is Him that helps you understand each other!

336

Anna's grandmother-in-law and Santi's grandmother, Raquel Moreira de Tejedo:

If you fight in the day, don't go to sleep right away. Make peace (with each other) and then in the morning, it will be marvelous.

337

Elizabeth's mother-in-law and Chad's mother, Glenda Miller:

- Never go to bed angry.
- Pray for each other.
- Be cheerful and happy, and say positive comments.
- Listen to each other tell stories that have been told before.
- Try to be positive of each other's families.
- Try to understand gender differences— "Men are from Mars, women from Venus."
- Pick your battles, and sometimes just let it go.
- Since we have retired, give each other space and patience.

338

Elizabeth's father-in-law and Chad's father, Randy Miller:

Glenda and I have been married thirty-five years. I married well above my level—she is almost perfect, and almost always happy, smiling, and will go along with almost anything. I do the following things to try to offset the sometimes difficult nature I can have.

1. I don't stifle her freedom, as long as we can afford it. I love it when she has people to meet, and places to go.
2. I pay all the bills, and handle all the business issues (such as tax prep) and mail.
3. I usually carry out all the trash.
4. She claims I snore, so we often sleep in separate beds. I always make my bed, and usually turn down her bed, and turn on her fan and light before she goes to bed.
5. I usually repair most of the broken things around the house, and arrange for repairmen when necessary.
6. I rid the yard of snakes and lizards when she goes semi-comatose about them.
7. I handle ordering all the meds for both of us, and try to ask each day if she has taken hers yet.
8. I wash all of my own clothes, and dry usually.

9. When she returns from the grocery, she calls, and I unlock the doors and usually bring in most of the bags. I try to get all of the large bulky items at the store (toilet paper, paper towels, water cases, cokes, and adult beverages, and heavy items).
10. I wash the dishes about half the time (since she did the cooking!).
11. We share mowing the yard. I hate mowing, but bought a gigantic mower that goes eleven miles per hour and cuts a wide swath, so that whoever has to do the chore, can do it in about two hours less than with the last riding mower we had! She has to be thankful for this.
12. I clean the toilets at least half the time.

None of these things do I always do, but I think, when I do them, they help her put up with me easier!

339

Elizabeth's sister-in-law and Chad's sister Jenny Elzen and her husband, Ethan:

These are some things that we've discovered over the past seven years that have made *our* marriage happy.

1. "They say" the first year of marriage and the first year of your first child's life are the hardest. I can't say I agree so much with the second part of that statement, but I know some couples that had a hard time adjusting to all the changes that came along with the addition of a little one. We had a *rough* first year of marriage, and I hate to see couples divorce during that first year. Stick out that first year and just see if things get easier. It did for us!

2. Don't go into marriage thinking divorce is an option. Don't threaten it during fights . . . it only opens up the possibility that it is an option.

3. Moving away from parents is an excellent thing to do the first year of marriage

to allow a couple the chance to rely on each other and make decisions together as a couple (without constant opinions from parents and in-laws).

4. Find time for each other each week . . . date night, whatever, especially when you have a child or children. This is *so important* for us. We also make sure not to talk about (our son) Palmer during this time together. We have the rest of the week to focus on him. This time is to focus on *us* (I've seen too many couples who realize they have nothing in common once the kids are grown and there is nothing else to talk about).

5. Find something you enjoy together (for us it's traveling) and something you enjoy doing without your spouse (for Ethan it's golf, for me it's shopping, getting a manicure-pedicure, lunch with friends).

6. Allow your spouse time with friends without feeling guilty for being without you.

7. Work stays at work. I tell Ethan that when he is home, I want him fully present. If he is going to spend the entire evening on his Blackberry, I'd prefer he stay at work.

8. Join a couple's Bible study group or another marriage-focused group. It makes you realize that other couples have experienced similar issues-problems during their marriage and to get advice and hear how they managed to get through it. It also can make your marriage seem fantastic after hearing how incredibly dysfunctional some are.

9. Men are physical and want to feel desired. Need I say more?

10. Choose your battles carefully. Figure out what is worth a fight and don't sweat the small stuff.

11. When your husband helps out with a child, do not criticize . . . even if it's the *complete* opposite of the way you would do it and it takes four times longer to do it (than it would take you). I've seen many dads refuse to do anything after being repeatedly criticized for not doing something the "right" way.

340

My brother, Charles Morton, who says he learned a lot from divorce:

Empathize with your spouse. Even if you do not think she should be upset-angry-hurt over something you have said or done, you can acknowledge to her that you see that she really is upset-angry-hurt. It goes a long way.

Knowing what makes a relationship strong is important: Be honest, no expectations, add to the relationship, don't keep score, and trust God.

341

My aunt, Lille Mortensen:

When looking for a husband, find a man with a wonderful disposition. Don't worry about how rich, how well educated, or how handsome. With a nice disposition everything else falls into place!

342

My cousin, Dave Mortensen:

Some people say marriage is a 50 percent–50 percent proposition. I think it is 80 percent–20 percent. Just remember, when you and your spouse have an argument, you are wrong 80 percent of the time!

He also shared these tidbits from a dinner party where the topic of happy marriages came up:

Really think about the person before you marry. Think about how your future spouse would fit in with your family and friends.

Make sure you know what's going on with the money!

Often it's what you don't say. Only talk out the points that are really important. If you fail to talk about important things, you are setting up trouble. But there is a lot you don't need to talk about.

Know where you agree and disagree!

Appreciate the sense of fun that you both share!

343

My cousin-in-law, Jan Mortensen:

When you are wrong, admit it. When you are right, don't rub it in.

(Added, in fun): Never go to bed angry. Stay up and throw things. (Ha, ha)

Advice from Experts

My friend Barbara Sanders, LCSW, has been a psychotherapist in private practice for almost twenty-five years and has been married almost twenty years herself. Here are some of her observations:

344

If something is bothering you, particularly in regard to your spouse, try to find a way to talk about the conflict in an unthreatening, calm manner, when not in the active conflict. There are all sorts of self-help books about how to fight effectively and how to communicate with your spouse. Don't be shy about asking a friend, a minister, or a professional for advice or recommendations way before the conflict festers and becomes a *huge* problem. Couples who can talk through conflict have the best chance at a healthy, happy marriage, and we all need to recognize that to be human is to be in conflict with our loved ones at times. There is nothing wrong or bad about that inherently, but it is what you do with it that matters.

345

When your spouse confuses you by something said or done, ask your spouse to clarify what happened if possible (at some point) so that you don't have to fantasize about what a certain word or phrase means. Fantasies are often a reflection of our worst fears, and the situation may grow into a catastrophe if left up to our ways of interpreting things. Might as well check it out earlier so as not to have to fret and worry so much. Give your spouse the respect to clarify the thing for themselves instead of your assuming you always know what was meant.

346

Find ways to have fun together, whether it be on a date, on a vacation, on the weekend, or any-time really. See if you can inspire yourself and your partner to be playful and enjoy yourselves instead of lapsing into a boring, blah lifestyle. On the other hand, treasure the calm and lov-ingly restful times with each other also, especially when life gets too hectic and fast-paced.

347

If affection with your spouse seems to de-crease over time, and this bothers you, find ways again to talk about it with your spouse or find ways you can encourage more affection, by giv-ing it rather than waiting for your spouse to initi-ate it, and perhaps resenting the wait.

R od Kochtitzky, a psychotherapist who specializes in working with couples, has drawn these "Marriage Maxims" mostly from his participation in the international community of Imago Relationship Therapists and the work of Harville Hendrix, who wrote the book *Getting the Love You Want: A Guide for Couples.*

Rod says that "about 40 to 50 percent of first marriages end in divorce. About 58 to 62 percent of second marriages end in divorce. Over 67 percent of third marriages divorce. Once you divorce you are emotionally and statistically more prone to divorce. We just go fall in love and end up in the same emotional power struggle with a different person." Here are Rod's "Marriage Maxims" derived and influenced by his work as a marriage counselor:

348

To have a lasting marriage one must always see their partner with eyes of appreciation and gratitude. If you can't, then you have conflict that needs to be worked on. Remember, conflict has more to do with the past than the present. Conflict does not have to be resolved. Some conflict cannot be. But conflict will stop you from loving in the present if you let it.

349

Without a vision, a relationship will perish. Because every couple is soooo different, every couple needs to build a conscious, common vision in order to thrive.

350

All couples (happy and unhappy, stable and unstable) have about the same number of problems they never solve (approximately 10). Once you solve a problem, another one magically takes its place.

351

Talking (often) makes many matters worse, not better. Listening makes matters better. God gave us two ears and one mouth for a reason! We need to listen twice as much as we talk to have a successful marriage. It is important that this work both ways.

352

Romance is spontaneous at the beginning; romance is a conscious and intentional act after the first three years or less. If you do not talk about it, plan it, and work together to make romance happen, it won't happen.

353

Be intentional about your relationship: For every one negative that happens, a loving couple will make sure five positives happen.

354

Two people who have grown apart *can* get reconnected.

355

Be conscious of your speech. "I feel that

you . . ." is not a feeling, it is most likely a judgment of your partner.

356

You can either be right or you can be in relationship, you choose. If you insist on being right, this means your partner is wrong and you should expect either distance or retribution.

357

In a conscious relationship, there is *no* shaming, blaming, accusing, judging, or criticizing. All shaming, blaming, accusing, judging, and criticizing are rooted in projection.

358

More money doesn't make you happier unless you are below poverty level.

359

Know twenty-five to thirty different behaviors that mean love to your partner. Do a different one every day.

360

The four transition points, how you say "good morning," "goodbye," "hello," and "goodnight" are powerful moments in the human psyche. Be aware of these magical moments and use them to enhance your connection. Staying distant during these transitions is the first step toward divorce.

361

No one can make you feel. No one can make you happy, sad, angry, or mad. Your partner might trigger a feeling in you. But it is your feeling—don't blame it on your partner and don't make yourself into a victim.

Rod noted that his maxims have also been influenced by writers such as Pat Love, John Gottman, and Terrance Real.

Marriage Tidbits from Mark and Susan DeVries (Co-authors of *The Most Important Year in a Man's Life/The Most Important Year in a Woman's Life*)

362

Most marriages are on a trajectory . . . either getting better or deteriorating. Marriages don't stay the same. As a wise old friend of ours has told us many times, "Untended fires soon become a pile of ashes.

Here are two of our favorite habits we've seen in marriages that are getting better:

363

The most valuable principle about building a thriving marriage we learned from John Gottman (of the University of Washington Love Labs). For us, his most profound principle was that friendship is the most important characteristic of happy marriages and that friendship between a husband and a wife gets built through a thousand strands of often meaningless conversation, more than through elaborate romantic getaways or over-the-top events.

364

The second habit we learned from our married children. Before their marriages, they made the decision to surround themselves with "marriage mentors," couples whose marriages they respected. They met with each marriage mentor at least once before the wedding, asking lots of questions, and discovering that there are surprisingly different ways of building a great marriage. Then, after the wedding, they kept in contact with their mentors, checking in at least once a year, structuring time to prevent their marriages from becoming stale.

Marriages that are getting worse are in a negative spiral of dissatisfaction, boredom, criticism, bitterness, resentment, defensiveness, and contempt—a spiral that can be painful, exhausting, and expensive. Marriages that are getting better do something deliberate to stay in a healthy, upward spiral. And those little inconveniences are, comparatively, exponentially less expensive and exhausting than the invest-nothing-and-hope-it-works-out alternative.

Prayer for a Married Couple

This prayer, written by Bishop Slattery in the 1800s soon after his marriage, was to be used each day in their family devotions at home in Boston:

365

O God, our heavenly Father, protect and bless us. Deepen and strengthen our love for each other day by day. Grant that by Thy mercy neither of us ever say one unkind word to the other. Forgive and correct our faults, and make us constantly to forgive one another should one of us unconsciously hurt the other. Make us and keep us sound and well in body, alert in mind, tender in heart, devout in spirit. O Lord grant us each to rise to the other's best. Then we pray Thee add to our common life such virtues as only Thou canst give. And so, O Father, consecrate our life and our love completely to Thy worship and to the service of all about us, especially those whom Thou hast appointed us to serve, that we may always stand before Thee in happiness and peace; through Jesus Christ our Lord. Amen

—*shared by Charles Morton*

Conclusion

In closing, I want to raise a toast to all of you who contributed your wisdom (and humor) to this book and to all of you who read it:

"May your troubles be less, may your blessings be more, and may nothing but happiness come through your door."

I truly hope that your marriages are happy, fulfilling, and lasting unions.

Notes